The **RANCHO GORDO**
HEIRLOOM BEAN
GROWER'S GUIDE

The **RANCHO GORDO**
HEIRLOOM BEAN
GROWER'S GUIDE

STEVE SANDO'S
50 FAVORITE VARIETIES

TIMBER PRESS

PORTLAND • LONDON

Photographs by Emma Alpaugh unless otherwise indicated.
Design: Jane Jeszeck/Jigsaw, www.jigsawseattle.com

Published in 2011 by Timber Press, Inc.

The Haseltine Building
133 S.W. Second Avenue, Suite 450
Portland, Oregon 97204-3527
www.timberpress.com

2 The Quadrant
135 Salusbury Road
London NW6 6RJ
www.timberpress.co.uk

ISBN-13: 978-1-60469-102-3

Printed in China

Library of Congress Cataloging-in-Publication Data
Sando, Steve.
    The Rancho Gordo Heirloom Bean Grower's Guide: Steve Sando's 50 Favorite
Varieties / Steve Sando. — First
        pages cm
    Includes bibliographical references and index.
    ISBN 978-1-60469-102-3
    1. Beans—Heirloom varieties—West (U.S) 2. Cooking (Beans) I. Title.
    SB327.S26 2011
    635'.65—dc22

                                            2010041467

A catalog record for this book is also available from the British Library.

Dedicated with love to my two sons,
Robert and Nico

Contents

THALASSA SKINNER, *CULTURE* MAGAZINE

Introduction:
My Love Affair with Beans

BEANS: WHO KNEW?

I started out growing heirloom tomatoes in the Napa Valley. After several careers behind desks and microphones, working outside and growing vegetables from seed was about the most thrilling thing I had ever done. My two small boys helped, mostly by getting in the way and reminding me how much I loved them—only making for a better workplace, in my mind. The whole process overwhelmed me, but I have the distinct memory of one afternoon toward the end of summer, sitting cross-legged in front of a cherry tomato plant. My youngest son, Nico, was sitting on my lap wearing nothing but droopy diapers. In the heat and silence, the two of us ravaged the poor tomato plant and ate every last ripe, red tomato. This was the payoff. After our "session," I looked and Nico's mouth was still full of blood red tomatoes and the dried juice and a few assorted seeds covered his cherubic torso. He couldn't speak yet, but everything was telling me this was a good career move, if I could somehow make it work.

Farmers markets in Napa are not a year-round thing. They start in March and end in November. Despite being in California, Napa has pipe-freezing cold winters and mostly mild springs and the soil is just not ready to produce great tomatoes until August. At the same time I was considering how to make this career move work, I was discovering dried heirloom beans, mostly from the Seed Savers Exchange and Native Seeds/SEARCH. Both groups are nonprofits and offer beans as seeds as well as by the pound. I remember eating my first bowl of Rio Zape beans and thinking I'd just tasted my future.

When I started out, I wasn't allowed to sell at my local Napa farmers market. Due to local politics, the management wanted to keep the market small and clubby. I had mostly tomatoes and the beans came later, but I didn't understand the politics or the culture of small town farmers markets. I thought I should be able to grow something locally and then sell it, but I guess it's more complicated than that. Unable to sell in Napa, I made my way up the Napa Valley to Yountville and their considerably smaller farmers market where I sold my tomatoes and later the beans. Now, you really need a large market to sell beans because most of the customers are there

Nico Sando helps at the Rancho Gordo trial gardens
STEVE SANDO

for tomatoes and cut flowers, despite their expensive market baskets and best intentions to eat lots of healthy vegetables. If only a small percentage would be buying dried beans, I needed a large market to make that small percentage count. Yountville wasn't the place, but the crowd was friendly and those early customers remain with me today, constantly reminding me of the old days.

One afternoon I received a call from the French Laundry, perhaps the most important restaurant in America. Eric Ziebold, the sous chef, had been shopping incognito and wanted to buy some beans for the French Laundry. I tried to sound professional on the phone as I did a "happy dance." Eric, who now runs City Zen in Washington, DC, brought Chef Thomas Keller to the market and I went one by one through the beans for them. Keller was an incredible listener and asked intelligent questions, which, thankfully, I was able to answer. After he left, people flocked to my booth asking which beans he was interested in.

One of Chef Keller's favorite beans is the Vallarta, a small solid yellow bean with a slight greenish cast and thick, rich texture. The Vallarta has remained a great success story over the years. Because Chef Keller wants it, we need to grow it— no matter how small a quantity. And because of this interest, everyone wants to know what the "Keller bean" is. A bean that really was on the brink of obscurity, if not worse, is thriving now.

I had been involved in seed-saving organizations and food advocacy groups, like Slow Food, but the success of the Vallarta bean really hit home for me: the best way to save these heirloom varieties was to eat them. Boring meetings with nonprofits will be the death of me. Everyone seems to blow out their chests in indignation and I just want to stand up and scream, "Shut up and eat!" I can't stand "moral food." Of course I want choices and education, but what I really want is something good to eat!

I haven't always been such a fanatic about beans. Growing up in California, they were always around. I appreciated them as something good to eat, especially with Mexican food. My family doesn't enjoy any Latin heritage, but California is a real melting pot and even though in our house a "nice dinner" meant steaks, abalone, Caesar salad, and gin martinis (it was the 1960s), school nights and rushed dinners were much more likely to be tacos than macaroni and cheese. In fact, I can't remember a single serving of mac and cheese as a child, making all the hype about the "blue box" all that much more confusing when I finally tried it as a young adult.

Our tacos were made of seasoned ground meat and a thick layer of canned Rosarita refried beans, cheese, and lettuce, more than likely knife-sliced iceberg. My father always claimed to doctor the beans up. I'm not sure what he did but I forever am addicted to the flavor of refried beans. Later, I learned to cook my own and mash and fry them myself and I've never looked back. I just love the flavor and the texture. I have one Mexican friend who was raised on Consteña brand refried beans from a can and he claims to prefer these to homemade, but his nostalgia might be ruling his palate. It is hard to believe someone would prefer the flavor of a canned bean.

I was reintroduced to beans as an adult when I started gardening. My first vegetable, like many home gardeners, was a tomato. After some success, I decided to spread my wings and try beans. Some networking with friends led me to Native Seeds, and later to the Seed Savers Exchange. Discovering the varieties of beans that were grown by gardening enthusiasts was like the first time I ate a Cherokee Purple heirloom tomato. The skies cleared, the heavens opened up, and I was eating well. Heirloom beans have been an obsession ever since.

Blue Speckled Tepary bean.
STEVE SANDO

Heirloom Beans:
Some Basic Bean Botany

Like heirloom tomatoes and other crops, heirloom beans are traditional varieties that have largely been passed over by industrial agriculture. Big ag has little use for a product that comes in seemingly endless variations; it's simpler and more cost-effective for growers to concentrate on the crops that are easiest to raise, harvest, and ship. So while the world has produced hundreds of varieties of beans over thousands of years, most of us have grown up seeing the same few types on the supermarket shelf from coast to coast: navy beans, black beans, garbanzos, pintos, and kidneys; dried for years, slow to cook and muted in flavor. No wonder beans are considered boring and bland by so many people, given such scanty choices and with all of them mass-produced!

Fortunately—for both our taste buds and biological diversity—a stubborn minority of home gardeners and small farmers has persisted in growing the old beans, even though they may not set as dense a crop or be as easy to harvest as the mass-market varieties. The locavore movement, emphasizing regional food production, and the rise in popularity of "farm-to-table" cooking have brought new customers for these traditional beans, 50 of which you can read about in this book. From the little Blue Speckled Tepary (it's not a lentil, despite a passing resemblance in shape) to the jumbo Snowcaps and gorgeously colored Mexican runners Ayocote Negro and Ayocote Morado, there's a universe of flavorful, richly textured heirloom beans to savor.

And because farmers who specialize in these beans tend to be smaller producers, they generally sell through each harvest. You're much less likely to find years-old heirlooms for sale, because chefs and home cooks alike are buying them up wherever they can find them.

What does this mean, to those of us brought up to believe that all dried beans are the same? For one thing, that these recently harvested heirlooms don't need anywhere near the soaking and cooking time we're used to allowing for those years-old supermarket brands. Often you can skip the soaking step entirely and still turn out a toothsome bean dish in just a couple of hours.

Secondly, with all the health benefits associated with beans, it's the taste and texture that makes them truly worth eating—and heirlooms offer a tantalizing array of choices, from dense and fudgy to creamy and light. Some taste potato-like, others are reminiscent of chestnuts. You could eat a different heirloom bean every day for months, each with its own distinctive character.

Another revelation is the pot liquor: heirlooms are so loaded with flavor that they actually create their own rich broth. Just add water! (And a bit of salt, when the time comes.) With beans this fresh, less truly is more; with just a handful of ingredients, you have a mouthwatering dish. You may even discover that fresher beans are easier to digest—I'm not promising anything, but we do have Rancho Gordo customers who report they experience less gas after eating heirlooms.

With few natural enemies and requiring little more than abundant water to cultivate, beans are a forgiving crop for the home gardener. You can even take a few beans from the bag of heirlooms you bought at the market, pop them in warm springtime soil and watch, like Jack in the fairy tale, as they sprout toward the sky. Maybe you don't have room for enough plants to produce dried beans for cooking, but the flowers will liven up your garden landscape and, if left to mature, will also produce seed for the next year's crop—or for trading with other seed savers. It's my firm belief that heirloom beans are as essential in the garden as they are on the table!

TYPES OF BEANS

The family Fabaceae is a large one, comprising a number of plants whose large seeds we call beans. The genus *Vigna* includes mung and adzuki beans, as well as black-eyed peas; *Vicia* gives us favas and the weedy vetches; *Glycene* is the soybean genus, and so on. Most of the heirlooms I love best—like the ones in this book—are in the genus *Phaseolus*. *Phaseolus* comprises a large variety of New World beans that fall into four main types: *P. vulgaris*, the so-called common bean; *P. acutifolius*, the tiny tepary; *P. lunatus*, the lima, which takes its Latin name from its half-moon shape; and *P. coccineus*, the runner bean.

Phaseolus vulgaris: Easy to grow, with a seemingly endless array of colors and textures, *P. vulgaris* accounts for the lion's share of my favorite pole and bush beans. Black, brown, yellow or white; spotted, dappled or marked with eyes; these reliable heirlooms are a pleasure in the garden and a delight to prepare and eat. Though the genus's Latin name dates back to ancient Europe, *Phaseolus* now denotes New World species.

Phaseolus acutifolius: The Americas' smallest bean, the tepary originated thousands of years ago in what are now the southwestern United States and Mexico. Ken Albala writes that teparies' small size is a direct

ANNABELLE LENDERINK

Delicious, Easy Heirlooms

Annabelle Lenderink is one of my favorite Bay Area farmers. She's been growing organically for more than 25 years, and she's well known around the region as the sales manager for the oldest continuously certified organic grower in California, Star Route Farms in west Marin County. Lenderink was a contributor to the *San Francisco Ferry Plaza Farmers' Market Cookbook*, and she's a real sweetheart. She also speaks half a dozen languages, which puts me to shame!

Since 1974, Star Route's glorious produce has become a mainstay of the best farmers markets and restaurant kitchens in San Francisco and neighboring counties. But Lenderink—like me—wanted to focus on heirloom varieties, including beans. On top of her full-time job, she started her own La Tercera Farm in Marin County, starting in Bolinas with a patch of land she leased from Star Route's owner, Warren Weber.

At La Tercera, Lenderink grows rare and unusual vegetables and herbs, many with old-fashioned European names like Marina di Chioggia (that's a squash) and Musquee de Provence (a pumpkin). Restaurants love her discoveries, buying up more than half of her crops; she also sells her produce at local farmers markets.

Lenderink has been growing fresh shelling beans for close to 20 years. "I got my first cranberry beans, and I just kept going from there," she says. "They're delicious, they're easy to grow; you just pick the pods and take them to market." Once there, the bean pods virtually sell themselves: "People love them, absolutely," Lenderink continues. "There's something about a fresh bean. And they're gorgeous pods, cranberries." They're also New World beans, originating in Colombia as the Cargamanto (see page 75).

Other traditional varieties Lenderink likes are the classic Italian Cannellini and French Flageolet. She also grows Black Coco beans, an obscure bush variety that can be eaten young as a snap bean, mature as a shelling bean, or dried—if you can find them to plant in the first place. "Black Cocos are beautiful even after they're cooked," she says. "When they're fresh, they're a shiny black-blue."

Lenderink grows her beans in northern Marin's Hicks Valley. "Bolinas is a little too foggy," she explains. But with enough sun, she adds, "They're reasonably easy to grow, given the right conditions: not too much heat, not too much fog; and they're not too demanding of nitrogen."

Lenderink's favorite way to prepare her fresh beans is a simple one: She cooks them up, and while they're hot she dresses them with vinegar, chopped garlic, salt, and pepper. It makes for a great warm salad, and the rest goes into the fridge for later. "It's an easy meal," says Lenderink—just what the hard-working farmer needs.

consequence of their ability to grow in the desert. Their ancient cultivators, the native Tohono O'odham people, bred them for productivity in a climate that would shrivel larger beans into indigestibility before they had the chance to mature. Tiny and tough, teparies have grown in dozens—if not hundreds—of varieties over the millennia; this book introduces just two of them, the Blue Speckled Tepary and the Brown Tepary. When preparing teparies, keep in mind that just because they're small doesn't mean they'll cook more quickly than other dried beans. They may be little, but they're dense.

Phaseolus lunatus: Originating in the Andes region of South America, the original limas got their name from the Peruvian port whence they were shipped to Spain beginning in the 16th century. These were large seeded limas; the smaller version is sometimes known as butter bean (see Florida Butter on page 93) or Baby Lima (page 57). The large-seeded, chestnut-flavored Christmas Lima and the Mexican red Baby Limas called Balero Teopisca are two more variations on the *P. lunatus* theme.

Phaseolus coccineus: Runner beans might just be my favorites. They're easy to grow and many of them have a lurid "cheap lipstick"–colored flower. You can eat the beans in all phases of growth, from flower to string beans to shelling bean and, perhaps best, as a dry bean. There are many claims that *P. coccineus* is the oldest cultivated legume in the New World, and with their ability to grow in cool or hot climates, it's no surprise. The plant sends off runners which can be trellised or allowed to run wild if you have the space. I've found it doesn't affect the yield, but it certainly looks neater in a home garden if you provide some support.

When is a "bean" not a bean? True beans belong to the family Fabaccac. Although the seeds of pods of other varieties of plants might resemble beans (cocoa beans, vanilla beans, coffee beans, castor beans, or even "Mexican jumping beans"), none of these is a true bean. Don't be fooled!

THE GROWING HABITS OF BEANS

A warm-weather crop, beans sprout quickly from seed, unfurling broad leaves that soak up both light from the sun and nitrogen from the atmosphere as their stems reach for the sky.

The growing habits of bean plants can vary widely. Some beans, like teparies, are tolerant of dry conditions, while most others require regular watering. A long growing season, with plenty of daylight hours, is essential for raising beans to their full maturity, when they can be saved dried for cooking and planting. But with a shorter season, you might still

be able to enjoy fresh snap and shelling beans, as long as you wait till the ground is well warmed before planting in spring.

Bean plants can have one of three growing patterns, each straightfor-wardly named: pole beans are high climbers that require support; runner beans send out long tendrils, or runners; and bush beans grow more com-pactly, without the need for trellising. Flowers can be white, pink, red or blue, and are followed by the development of green pods that, if left unpicked, develop beans that can be eaten fresh or dried to maturity.

Most beans are self-pollinating hermaphrodites. Each bush and vine blooms with flowers containing both male and female parts, enabling them to set fruit on their own without having to depend on pollen from another plant. This self-reliant quality has helped heirloom bean varieties to retain their individual characteristics over the millennia. Bean historian Ken Albala writes that archaeologists have unearthed bean plants thousands of years old that, while appearing very different from their modern-day counterparts, are nonetheless genetically similar. So when you plant an heirloom bean or seedling today, you're cultivating a plant with deep roots indeed!

LEFT *A pole bean climbs up a stalk of red amaranth.*
STEVE SANDO

RIGHT *Scarlet runners, named for their red flowers.*
STEVE SANDO

Beans of the New World and Beyond

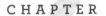

Early on I decided to focus on beans native to the New World. I don't think we've been particularly good neighbors to the countries to our south and I wanted to see if in some small way I could change a few minds. I wanted to encourage people to think of us all as *the Americas*—we have more in common than most people think. Food seemed like a natural common ground, so I made saving New World varieties a priority.

I've had people roll their eyes about heirloom beans, thinking it's a little precious or perhaps a desperate attempt to hitch my wagon to the heirloom tomato craze. I've also met people who think my obsession is cute or admirable and not much more. All I can suggest is that you actually eat some of the heirlooms listed in this book. Very few are chosen because of their looks alone. I grow most of them because their flavor and texture are remarkable and the world would be a sadder place without them.

I have friends who have been aware of my work with Rancho Gordo and seed saving for years and only just recently decided to actually eat them. Most often, their reactions are almost of disbelief. How can beans taste so good? They've been humoring me all these years. It's a reminder to me that I can go on and on about the taste of the beans but it's not until someone actually eats them that they really understand the difference. Oddly, young cooks who don't have a lot of the same cultural associations with beans that many of us in the older generation have are the most open-minded. When I meet an old-time bean person, I often have to take a defensive stance. They're bean lovers, but they're also very set in their ways and insist on all sorts of elaborate steps to cooking beans, often involving chicken stock and ham bones. I love these folks, but they usually have only been exposed to old beans from the supermarket.

I remember being in Rome and sitting at a friend's family table. The mother had created and incredible meal with gnocchi, meats, salads, and wine. I was fairly young and impressionable but I knew I was in for a treat. As the gnocchi were served, everyone commented on how beautiful they were and the smell of the ragu made them all the more attractive. "My mother's gnocchi are as light and delicate as the wings of a butterfly!" my friend boasted. I took a bite and indeed they were delicious. I'd only had gnocchi a few times but these seemed great and I loved the deep, rich sauce that covered them. Apparently the family wasn't so impressed. There was only silence and from the mother, a sense of shame. "I'm so sorry. I wasn't paying attention." Apparently they were too heavy and leaden. What did I know?

One result of having a monoculture like Italy's is that everyone can agree on what makes good gnocchi. I assume it can be oppressive if you're trying to break free from tradition, but you save a lot of time not arguing about food and culture. Things are understood.

Here in the United States, we have a huge variety of tastes; ranging anywhere from Mario Batali's Babbo restaurant in New York to the Olive Garden. We can't seem to agree on anything as far as food goes. On top of that, we only seem to be interested in the cultures of our shared European ancestors and not in the cultures of our neighboring nations to the South. How is it we've been such poor neighbors with Mexico and Latin America? Quick: name at least one Egyptian pharaoh. Now, name one Mayan king. I bet King Tut or Ramses came to mind pretty easily but you're still struggling to name a Mayan. I don't think you're alone.

There was an initiative in the 1930s called the Good Neighbor policy. Instituted by Franklin Roosevelt in a time of growing conflict, the ultimate goal may have been cynical— to gain influence in Latin America, or maybe just to get our bananas cheaper, but the idea was a good one. We don't live in Europe. For many of us, our European ancestors are generations away. Since we now live in the New World, why not embrace the cultures around us? I love the concept of the Americas. From Canada to Chile, the real cultural influences over the last generations have come from here. We're still defining our culture and ourselves as Americans. Of course, the European roots that many of us share area significant factor in who we are, but just as important is our shared history with our neighbors in the Americas and our sense of place on this continent.

As far as being neighborly, we've done a horrible job at times. Some of our trade policies have been a disaster, creating the very situations that send desperate people to the borders, looking for refuge in the United States. Or maybe we open a factory, hire locals, and then close it as soon as China seems like a better deal. How neighborly is that? Less serious but no less offensive is the behavior of some tourists who visit places like Cabo or Cancun during spring break only to party, and disrespect the Mexican people and the rich cultural heritage of their country while they are at it.

We can argue until the cows come home about how to solve the drug problems, the border wars, and illegal immigration. Obviously they're complex issues. We've had a hand in creating some of the problems, and have a responsibility to address them beyond closing the borders to stop illegal immigration.

I do think one area of common ground that we all can agree on is food. The food that was created in the New World—the Americas—changed the Old World and continues to help define our culture. If politics bore you, you can at least agree that the world is a better place for a nice slice of an heirloom tomato. Maybe I'm naive, but I'd like to define who we are with a broader border. A tomato has its roots in Mexico, but it traveled well and developed into the glorious fruit we have all over the world today. Beans changed less, but they also were great travelers. Can you imagine Mexican food without refried beans? How about a French cassoulet without big, white runner beans? Or British beans and toast without the beans? These foods have their origins in the Americas, but are culturally neutral. Focusing on this fact is a step toward being a better neighbor.

I'm not even beginning to suggest that we take up a New World diet exclusively. But it is interesting to look at what the Mesoamericans were eating before the European conquest: it was a diet incredibly rich in good, healthy food. The Europeans introduced dairy, rendered fat, and wheat into a diet that was based primarily on chiles, beans, and corn. It's worth looking at these ingredients and the diet they comprised. The cultures the Europeans found when they hit New World shores were incredibly advanced in some key areas like astronomy, mathematics, and agriculture—there are things we can still learn from them. While I wouldn't want to do without my carnitas of deep fried pork, I do wonder how well I would do on a pre-Hispanic diet.

This is why I focus on New World food. I have friends who think I'm nuts and others who are curious, but it's a perspective I like. Maybe it won't change the world, but maybe it's a step in the right direction for a modern Good Neighbor policy.

BEANS IN THE NEW WORLD

Wild ancestors of our common bean, *Phaseolus vulgaris*, have been found throughout all of Mesoamerica, in the Andes, and as far south as Argentina. Ken Albala, in his engaging and thorough 2007 book *Beans: A History*, writes that the residents of what are now Mexico and Peru were the first to domesticate the bean, but it's hard to pinpoint exactly when. Tropical humidity hasn't been helpful in dating ancient beans, but domestication likely occurred around 6,000 BCE and possibly even earlier. Whatever the date, this was a key step in the development of early American civilization. These original peoples were largely vegetarians with beans, corn, chiles, and squash making up the bulk of their diet. Without much meat available, you can see how important the beans must have been: Eaten with

Eye of the Goat beans.
STEVE SANDO

whole-grain corn to supply the right complementary amino acids, they would have created a complete protein source. Had there been no beans for them to eat, would the Aztec, Maya, and Olmec cultures have become so advanced centuries before their first contact with Europeans? We can only wonder.

But it's surely no accident that in the early farming technique known as "the three sisters," farmers would plant corn, beans, and squash together so that the cornstalks furnished a natural trellis for the beans to climb, while the spreading leaves of the squash acted to keep down weeds around the roots of all three crops. Not only did the three plants team up to reduce human labor in the field, but when eaten together they provided a well-balanced meal.

Once introduced, bean cultivation quickly traveled north, where Native Americans adopted many of the same methods developed by their Mesoamerican counterparts. Along with the southern beans, North American natives had their own tepary (*Phaseolus acutifolius*) in the Southwest. Tiny teparies thrive in arid conditions, which made them a key crop where water was scarce.

The "discovery" of the New World introduced Europeans to a cornucopia of native foods, including beans, which the Old World quickly took to its heart—and then reintroduced to their native land via successive waves of colonists, settlers, and later immigrants. So a bean with a lineage that reaches back to prehistoric South America might resurface in any number of Yankee dishes, from slow-baked bean pots—with or without "franks"—to savory soup recipes from virtually every European food tradition.

While beans are among what you could call the founding foods of this great landmass of ours, they also bear a heavy historical burden as a result of the Great Depression, when meat was scarce on the American table. If you are of a certain age, you might well be used to associating beans with hard times and poverty. At the farmers markets, I have met so many senior citizens who laugh and shake their heads about having to eat beans during the Depression, and then wistfully ask if I have this or that old-fashioned bean they remember from those dark days.

It seems that as soon as times were good, most Americans dumped the habit of bean eating, except in regional pockets like the Southwest and the deep South. Even in Boston, which may have earned its "Beantown" moniker in the colonial era because of the locally produced molasses that flavored traditional baked beans (or maybe because Bostonians were known to be tight with a dollar), you seldom see them on restaurant menus.

Beans also suffer from what I call the *Blazing Saddles* stigma, after the—admittedly hilarious campfire-flatulence scene in that 1974 Mel Brooks movie, which completely wiped out any progress toward popular acceptance that beans might have made over the decades since the Depression ended.

But in the 21st century, I'm happy to say, Americans are rediscovering the joys of old-fashioned beans—and this time around, they're seeing the bean in its myriad varieties as an affordable delicacy rather than a humble, monotonous staple. Bean-eaters of today, you can hold up your heads in pride: these heirlooms are as American—and as tasty!—as apple pie made with fruit straight from the orchard.

BEANS IN OTHER LANDS

Beans from the New World were quickly adapted to European farms and kitchens, especially by the Italians—think of hearty pasta e fagioli and mouthwatering minestrone. But it's too easy to sell France, Spain, and

MARIA

Planting the Seeds of the Rancho Gordo-Xoxoc Project

I always say I first met Maria Bisma through her beans. My Mexican business partners Yunuen Carrillo Quiroz and Gabriel Cortés Garcia had met her at a local market and immediately sent me a sample of her harvest after they had cooked a pot of her Rebosero beans for themselves. Almost a mottled mauve, the beans are unlike any others I'd seen. "Wait until you cook them," said Gabriel's mother, Chavela. "You won't believe the flavor and the rich caldo they make."

I wasn't too concerned about their flavor; I wanted to get them because of their looks. If they tasted great, all the better. I made them, as I always do with a new bean, with onion, garlic, and olive oil. I salted about three quarters of the way through and of course I used a good clay pot. Now the reality is that there are some beans that are just pretty and showy, and that's fine but the flavor is nothing to write home about. Then there are the beans that are so delicious it reminds me of why I do what I do. Maria's Reboseros were the point of all this hard work! They're somewhat creamy but they're also somehow meaty and with their thin skins, they release an unreal pot liquor.

On my next trip down to Mexico, Yunuen and Gabriel had arranged a meeting with Maria. We had to drive quite a long way and the last part of the trip was up a winding road that seemed to never quit. Being really rural, it wasn't paved and the journey was pretty rough going. Maria's compound was simple but neat. Maria herself was a short little dynamo who couldn't understand what this gringo was doing in her house. She understood that he said he loved the beans, but it all seemed a little odd to her. I don't blame her. I had my then ten-year-old son Robby with me, and she immediately sat us down to lunch. Of course there were beans (her Reboseros), made all the more delicious by the handmade tortillas from corn Maria had grown. We also had a nice soup and some great goat barbecue. She had cola for Robby but the rest of us drank water. She insisted we sit but she kept fussing about as we visited. She showed us her baskets and it turns out that in her spare time she makes them from local reeds.

"I was the least pretty of all of my sisters and my father felt sorry for me," she told us. "My sisters all married well but I got the beans and in the end, I think I've been the lucky one." Maria knew she could count on the beans year after year, as a food for herself and to sell at market. Once she's harvested her beans, Maria takes them down to the local *tianguis* (market) to sell. She can only take about 20 kilos because the trip on foot is five miles down the hill and she has to carry a scale as well.

Maria has someone come plow her field at the beginning of the season, but otherwise she does everything by herself—from planting, to irrigation, to weeding, and finally harvesting and cleaning. She has no money for pesticides or herbicides, so her technique is beyond what we would consider organic. She doesn't have a lot of extra stock and what she does have she sells quickly, so she doesn't have to worry much about bugs.

I was exhausted just meeting her and the thought of all the work she was doing made it worse. How was it possible? Here was a tiny In-

A santo from Puebla.

dian woman in her sixties and she was going like gangbusters. She gave us a tour of her fields and I noticed she'd constantly stop to pick up stray beans that had gathered here and there. She'd show me and then pocket the beans in her skirt. No movement was wasted. If she was going to bend down, she was going to collect seeds for later. She showed us some corn and squash and even a few potatoes but clearly her love was the beans. After a walk around the field, she insisted on showing us her water source and proving that it was clean, in case we doubted her. "Black water" is an issue in Mexico now as some questionable sewage is being used to irrigate dry, thirsty fields. I saw it in Hidalgo but I'd have to assume it was a problem in other parts of the country as well. Maria would have no part of it and she pays for access to a local well. She insisted I drink the water and of course my defenses went up. How do I explain to this sweet old woman that I was concerned about drinking water in Mexico and that even if her water were pure as snow, I still had concerns? I couldn't do it. She was so proud; I just took a big gulp and smiled. It was warm and not very pleasant but I knew Maria had something to prove to me so I just went for it.

Maria uses a donkey to make rows and to plant the seeds. This is tough work because it can take a few seasons before the donkey, or even a horse, gets the hang of it.

Maria grows two other beans but it's the Rebosero beans that are the star. In Mexico, most people have a love of beans, but as the old mercados and tianguis become more trouble to manage and shop, and the Wal-Marts and superstores become more convenient, beans like the Rebosero are destined to fade into obscurity.

While there's room for the Wal-Marts and all the convenience they offer, I don't understand why it always has to be an all or nothing venture. Wouldn't it be great if some of these big superstores could buy from the Marias of the world as well? Or maybe just figure out a clever way to help Maria thrive along with their industrial offerings? It won't be easy but it's not impossible. And really, there's no way a large industrial grower could challenge the flavor that Maria gets with her crops.

Maria's daily life is a lot of work, but she has a lot of ambition and energy. Her disposition was sunny and almost carefree; but she was alone, and I couldn't help but feel a little sorry for her. I could tell she loved the idea of going to market with her goods, and I'm sure it helped fill some social voids in her life. I didn't feel comfortable prying into her personal life, but her village, like many throughout Mexico, seemed to be missing men, especially younger ones.

When I got home, I put Maria's beans on the Rancho Gordo website. I remember it was a Friday night and I may have sent out a Twitter announcement or an email. Monday morning, we arrived to a flood of orders. We'd oversold Maria's beans! I quickly contacted Yunuen and told her that we needed a lot more beans from Maria for the next season. A few weeks later I received a call from Yunuen. She had seen Maria and given her the news.

It turns out that Maria's grandson, who had been planning the dangerous and illegal trip north to the United States, decided to stay and help his grandmother raise beans. I started welling up when I heard this news. Could this really be a side effect of our Rancho Gordo-Xoxoc Project? I wanted the beans selfishly, and the end result is my customers get to try these delicious beans and Maria gets to have her grandson working with her on their land growing their heritage beans. How could it be so easy? I decided then and there that governments and nonprofits all have their roles but providing a way for small businesses to work with other small businesses is a vital piece to the puzzle. The puzzle can be immigration reform, the economy, or just being a good neighbor. So many seem to benefit without a lot of work!

Portugal short: all of these great European cuisines have excellent bean dishes, from the classic French cassoulet to Iberian bean-and-kale soups.

Whether regional specialties or sources of national pride, bean dishes have made their way into the food traditions of most cultures. Even in northern latitudes where the days may never get long enough to grow even favas to full maturity, beans are eaten fresh when young or imported, dried and canned, from sunnier climes.

Ancient bean varieties originating outside the Americas include those favas (*Vicia faba*). Also known as broad beans, they may have been gathered in the wild, in what would become the Holy Land, even before the Mesoamericans domesticated *Phaseolus vulgaris* and *Phaseolus acutifolius* in the Andes and Mexico.

Peas, chickpeas, and pigeon peas (of the genera *Pisum*, *Cicer*, and *Cajanus*, respectively) and lentils (*Lens culinaris*) are similarly ancient legumes. They're believed to have originated in the Fertile Crescent region of western Asia, which includes the traditional growing regions of Mesopotamia and the Levant: hummus was born here.

In India, as Ken Albala points out, a largely vegetarian population of Hindus and Brahmins has ensured that legumes never suffered from the association with poverty and low estate with which European and American cultures have saddled them. Some of the world's tiniest beans, those in the genus *Vigna* (of which the mung bean, *V. radiata*, is probably the best known), originated here.

Larger and sweeter than other vignas, the ruby-red adzuki bean (*V. angularis*) is eaten chiefly by the Chinese and Japanese, who use it in everything from soups to desserts. Its African cousin *V. unguiculata* (the black-eyed pea) made its way to Europe via Greece in ancient times, but in our day remains associated with the cuisine of African-Americans whose ancestors, sold into slavery, carried seed-beans with them from their native continent.

Perhaps planet Earth's most influential legume, soy (*Glycine max*) could be viewed as the success story of the bean world—or as a poster child for overexposure. There's a reason "heirloom soybean" is virtually an oxymoron: from its roots in China some three millennia ago, this bean has been cultivated and genetically tweaked into a crop its wild ancestors would barely recognize. Long favored as a meat substitute when compressed into tofu or fermented to make miso or tempeh, soy got a steroidal dose of mass-market appeal in the late 20th century with reports that its health benefits could include the relief of menopausal symptoms and other ills. Virtuous as it may be nutritionally, the soybean tastes pretty terrible when cooked like other dried beans; that's why, except for the fresh green beans called edamame, it's almost always processed into some other form before it's fit to eat. Give me a New World heirloom any day!

THE HEALTH BENEFITS OF BEANS

Most people have at least a vague understanding of the health benefits of beans: They're loaded with protein and fiber and when teamed with the right carbohydrates, they form a complete protein source—no need for meat. Beans are high in calcium, low in saturated fat and sodium, and very low in cholesterol. Because they help to regulate blood sugar and blood pressure, beans are also beneficial for people with diabetes and hypertension. These are all great virtues—and that's the problem: a lot of people's eyes glaze over when they hear about the health benefits of beans. You say calcium, and they hear tedium. They want something delicious and exciting and say, "Aren't there enough vitamins in my breakfast cereal to carry me through the day? Why do I need more health food?" The fact is, beans can be delicious and exciting, with very little effort required to turn out a savory side dish or soup. Of course, you can go to more elaborate lengths to incorporate beans into your meals; but why go to the trouble? Dieticians and others in the health industry can have a tendency to take things a little too far when they discover a superfood like beans. As if there weren't enough tasty ways to enjoy beans as beans, these innovators have to engineer them into everything: bean flour, sweet bean pies, bean cutlets. I wouldn't advocate a lack of imagination in the kitchen, but we Americans tend to go overboard when we see every superfood as a cure-all. We cram it into everything we can think of until we're sick of it. My hunch is that if you tried eating only beans, blueberries, pomegranates, and oatmeal, you'd be back on the junk food before you could say "boo."

Beans should be part of a well-balanced diet—not always the main event, but a daily presence like vegetables or fruit. I can't think of too many meals that wouldn't benefit from at least a little side serving of savory beans. I have small glass ramekins I like to use. These are especially handy if you have fussy eaters (also known as children) who don't like their foods to mix, or if you're entertaining a wary diner who's not so sure about this bean thing. Another bonus with ramekins or other individual small serving bowls is that your guests can enjoy their beans "soupy" or drier, as they prefer.

So let's ignore beans as a main dish for the moment. What is the nutritional boost of serving a quarter cup of cooked beans along with your regular meal? Suppose you had a nice roast chicken, a vegetable, a salad, and some beans? What do beans bring to the plate?

"They're super high in fiber, they're super high in protein, they're low in the 'three C's': cholesterol, calories, and cost," says Napa chef, nutritionist, and caterer Karen Schuppert, who loves the wide choice of varieties and textures among heirloom beans—not to mention their versatility. "The advantage to heirlooms is they really do have more of a distinctive flavor, they aren't mass-produced, and they aren't dried like little pebbles," she continues. "They are a mainstay in my kitchen: I use them in so many different types of recipes." Schuppert adds beans with brown rice to her fish tacos: The whole grain supplies the amino acids that beans need to form a complete protein source. She also uses heirlooms in her salads. "I always keep a cup of cooked beans at hand," she says, and she sprouts heirlooms as well: "Sprouted is just a wonderful way to enjoy their flavor and health benefits."

A certified nutrition educator who trained at Bauman College, which specializes in holistic nutrition and culinary arts, Schuppert is as enthusiastic about the healthy side of beans as I am about their flavor and texture—and that's saying a lot. She's also great at explaining why these tasty legumes are so good for you. "The starches in the beans are what help to keep everything digesting slowly—they act kind of like a sponge," Schuppert says. "You don't get the spikes in blood sugar that you do with foods you absorb more quickly." That's why beans are good for diabetics, who often struggle with fluctuating blood-sugar levels that can have serious health consequences. The high fiber content of beans makes them heart-healthy, and along with those slow-digesting starches, also help to provide a feeling of fullness, making them a terrific diet food: "You're satiated, so therefore you're not likely to eat as much—they're filling, but still low in calories," Schuppert explains.

But wait, there's more! "We always think of fruits and vegetables as high in antioxidants, but beans are also high in antioxidants and in vitamins—B vitamins in particular," she continues. Why does this matter? Antioxidants help protect our cells from breaking down, or oxidizing, while B vitamins are essential to the human diet and must be replaced every day. So even a side serving of beans adds more than flavor, color, and texture to your meal—it supports your body in a number of important ways.

But imagine now that your main course is a simmering bean and kale soup, with or without meat or rice. Increasing your serving of beans to a half a cup or even three quarters of a cup means a huge nutritional bang that's hard to ignore. So, what if over a week you have a small serving of beans each day as a side dish, except for two or three meals where beans are the stars? It's not hard to do, and it's delicious. Depending on how many people you're planning to serve, you can cook up a cup or two in the morning, or even in the afternoon—remember, recently-harvested heirlooms don't need anywhere near the amount of soaking and cooking time required by mass-produced beans—and, at mealtime, finish them any number of ways: with a squeeze of lime, a dash of hot sauce or salsa, a dollop of yogurt, a sprinkle of cheese, or even all of the above. Chopped onion? Shredded lettuce? Cilantro? Tomato? Why not? You can mix your beans with rice, as Schuppert does, for tacos, or to stuff a pepper, or just as a side. You can mash them into refried beans, puree them with spices to make a dip, stir them into a soup or chili. Beans make a hearty and sustaining breakfast, with or without some eggs and toast. With all of the heirloom varieties now available, you can have a different bean, prepared a different way, every day for weeks and never get bored.

Not only are these versatile beans both tasty and healthy; they represent a ridiculously easy way to reduce our carbon footprint by occasionally replacing resource-heavy meats with a more sustainable protein. In terms of natural resources, energy, and labor, bringing a pound of beans to market takes a lot less than producing a pound of beef—and that's not even

Salsa from the trial garden.
STEVE SANDO

counting transportation, which we tend to assume is what causes much of the emissions. You don't have to take my word for this: "Food-Miles and the Relative Climate Impacts of Food Choices in the United States," a 2008 study out of Carnegie Mellon University's civil engineering department, found that food *production* alone—before shipping—accounts for 83 percent of the greenhouse gases emitted in the process of feeding the average American household, with red meat far outweighing other food categories in the amount of emissions produced.

The study's authors, Christopher L. Weber and H. Scott Matthews, concluded that because transportation accounts for so little of the total greenhouse gases caused by our diet—just 11 percent, with less than half of that emitted in the final delivery to retail—Americans could more easily reduce their emissions by relying just a little bit less on red meat, wherever it is raised, than by following the "locavore" policy of buying groceries from nearby producers. "Shifting less than one day per week's worth of calories from red meat and dairy products to chicken, fish, eggs, or a vegetable-based diet"—like beans, I must interject!—"achieves more greenhouse gas reduction than buying all locally sourced food," they wrote in the journal *Environmental Science and Technology*.

I'm certainly not advocating a meatless lifestyle unless it makes sense for you. I'm just suggesting that beans should be a more important part of our diet than the traditional beef, for a lot of reasons. There's room at the table for all the ingredients; but it's hard for beans, so long associated with poor times and flatulence, to compete with the advertising budgets of the beef industry. I would respectfully argue that the roles of beans and beef should be reversed. We'd all be healthier—including the planet.

The trial gardens
at Rancho Gordo.
STEVE SANDO

Growing the World's Most Delicious Beans

Fast-growing, attractive, and productive, beans are a terrific plant for virtually any home gardener, from the timid beginner to the greenest of thumbs. And unlike so many crops that pull nutrients from the ground in which they grow, bean plants are actually good for the soil, because they transform atmospheric nitrogen into the biological form that's essential for nourishing plant life. It's not by accident that so many Napa Valley wine-grape growers plant fava beans as a cover crop while the vines are resting for the winter. When spring comes, vineyard workers till the plants into the soil as a nutritious green manure. You can do the same, with the added attraction of having tasty, fresh favas to snack on at a time of year when few other garden crops are anywhere near ready to eat.

The life of a bean is pretty wild. The plant germinates from a seed very quickly and then starts a miraculous growth. Beans are great for beginning gardeners because you can almost watch them grow. A gardener who had one of those bean plants that wouldn't stop growing surely wrote the story about Jack and his magic beanstalk.

After the plant is established and has lots of true leaves, it produces a flower, which is followed by a miniscule bean pod. The pod grows, finally resembling what we know as a string bean. You can obviously enjoy green beans if you like, but remember you'll have to remove the strings along the side the way our grandparents used to do. The beans in the pod are still white and small at this point, but that changes quickly—they transform into any number of incredible colors as they dry. When the pods are mature, you stop watering; the plant dies, and the pods go from lush and green to tan and brittle.

PREPARING YOUR GARDEN FOR BEANS

Readying a garden bed is like preparing to have company: you want to be the perfect host or hostess. You want to make your guests feel welcome, and you want to do all that is in your power to make their stay with you as enjoyable as possible. Sometimes, however, with all the cooking, cleaning, and preparations, you burn out before the guests even arrive. The same

Black runner bean plant in flower.
STEVE SANDO

thing can happen with your garden bed. You could obsessively prepare the perfect plot, but at what cost?

With that in mind, let's get ready to grow some beans! Site selection should be first on your to-do list: A spot that receives six to eight hours of sunlight a day would be your first choice. And don't feel you have to hide your beans away, just because they're food crops. Some bean plants are incredibly gorgeous and the runner varieties all have exceptional flowers, so you may want to take that into account when selecting your site. Nothing looks healthier or more abundant than a bean plant climbing up a trellis. Add blooms and pods, and you have something wonderful to look at as well as to eat. The decision to go organic or not is a big one for most home gardeners, but beans are pretty easy. If you keep them watered and fed,

Bean weevils at work.

you shouldn't have many problems. The biggest trouble is weevils. I freeze all of my beans from the trial garden for three days and it kills any pests and their eggs and it hasn't affected germination. If cutworms are making trouble in your garden, try a dusting of *Bacillus thuringiensis* as an alternative to pesticides.

If you are readying your soil specifically for beans, there are a couple of things to keep in mind. Beans prosper in soil with a pH of 6.0 to 6.8. Check with your local community college, gardening club, or nursery for where to get a soil sample tested, or purchase a do-it-yourself home kit from your local nursery or online. There is also a very simple test you can do at home, and all you need is baking soda. If you wet a soil sample, add a pinch of baking soda, and the mix fizzes, your soil may be too acidic for beans and other crops (remember third grade and the vinegar-baking soda volcano?) You could also do nothing, and your beans will probably be just fine. Just keep in mind that beans don't need a great deal of nitrogen; too much, and they'll grow mainly foliage and very few pods.

If you do need to lower the acidity, you can add dolomitic limestone (2½ to 10 pounds per 100 square feet). Heavy clay soil may require a bit more. To reduce the acidity even further, you can till the limestone into the top 6 inches of soil. To raise the pH by about one unit, you can try adding wood ash from your fireplace. The ratio is about 5 to 10 pounds per 100 square feet. This technique has been used in Mexico for hundreds of years, and clearly the Mexican people know a thing or two about growing beans.

You may also need to amend your soil with nutrients. Depending on your garden site, you may need to amend the soil heavily; or, in some rare

Looking for beans among the weeds.

cases, not at all. It is a personal decision, one best made after consulting experienced gardeners in your neighborhood; because they are probably dealing with the same soil issues and microclimates, they are your best resource. When deciding how to amend, budget can be a factor as well. One could spend a small fortune purchasing fancy composts and trendy amendments, but how much better could an heirloom bean be? If you amend your soil with the neighbors' horse manure (thoroughly composted to avoid weeds) and feed it every two to three weeks with a homemade and virtually free compost tea, you should have a bumper crop.

In addition to bean weevils and cutworms, some beans are prone to predators such as the Mexican bean beetle, aphids, leafhoppers, and spider mites. Downy mildew is a principal disease. Remember, the plants will naturally fight these enemies and become stronger for it. Pests and disease don't like a strong plant.

Many farmers inoculate their beans before planting. This allows the bean seed to provide its own nitrogen. Some of the old timers soak beans in milk overnight to make them sprout faster. You could do a couple testing plants to prove or disprove these practices. Or again, you could do nothing and have fabulous beans.

At our trial gardens, I don't presoak the beans. I just direct-seed them after any danger of frost has passed. I make rows about two feet apart and plant every six or seven inches. I've rushed to plant on the first safe frost-free day and I've waited until late June to give the soil a chance to warm up and noticed no real difference. I used to panic and think I had to plant them all at once, but the reality is that the soil is ready when it's ready and there's not a whole lot you can do about it.

A lot of home gardeners still practice the "three sisters" method—planting corn as a trellis for beans and squash to keep down the weeds—but I haven't had much luck with squash as a weed suppressant. Nothing short of elbow grease has worked for me.

BEAN TRELLISING, A TO Z

Nature is full of vining plants with the competitive advantage of being able to climb to the tops of larger plants and seek out light. In the world of beans, there was a time when all beans behaved this way. Today, we have bush and runner beans to choose from in addition to pole beans, for which we have the fun task of building a trellis.

In the home garden, trellises don't just give your bean tendrils something to cling on to; they can also bring a unique look and feel to your landscape. There are endless configurations that would serve the purpose of holding up your beans through the end of the season. If you are anything like me, once you start playing with different configurations, you won't be able to walk through the hardware store without scheming up some new designs.

Use the following ideas as a guide to get you started. Just like building compost, the best result will come from using the materials that are available to you. If you are a welder or a woodworker, you may want to build something more elaborate than the simple zip-tie and wood frame designs below. Then again, if your toolbox has been gathering dust for a while, this should help you get started growing pole beans.

Pole beans on a trellis in the Rancho Gordo trial garden. Trellises can be structured in various ways; this one combines several X-type frames.
STEVE SANDO

MATERIALS

- 8 foot plant stakes
- zip-ties
- twine

THE A-FRAME

1. Lay a stake on the ground as a guide for where you plan to build the trellis.

2. Push two sets of stakes a foot (or as far your soil will allow) into the ground a few inches from the end of the stake and about one foot apart.

3. Allow the stakes to cross at the top, pick up the stake from the ground, set it on top of where the two supports cross, and wrap a zip-tie around that intersection.

4. Now you can push stakes into the ground every 8 inches or so, filling in the structure. You can extend the trellis with new top stakes as needed.

5. If you want to use less wood, leave a gap in your vertical stakes, add a stake a couple of inches from the ground, and run twine between that and the top bar.

THE X-FRAME

This frame is similar to the A-frame, but instead of crossing the stakes at top, intersect them in the middle. Use twine as an option here by adding horizontal stakes at both the top and bottom.

THE MV-FRAME

1. Start by making an "M" by following steps 1–3 for building an A-frame, then repeating so that you basically have two A-frames side-by-side.

2. At the point where your two A-frames intersect a few inches off the ground, attach a horizontal stake. Run twine from one of the top bars down and around the bottom bar, then up to the other top bar to create the "V."

You can also use stakes in place of the twine. When using twine, I suggest starting with a few vertical stakes at each end, so that the top bar is nice and sturdy. Remember, this thing needs to stand up for at least a few months during the growing season.

OTHER TRELLIS IDEAS

If simply rolling out some plastic netting sounds more appealing to you than all that tying of twine, a number of products are available from farm and garden suppliers. Try to find something with about a 4-inch grid that you can reach your hand through. Zip ties work great for securing that netting to any stout structure.

Rebar frames

Another interesting option is to incorporate rebar. I have had success bending 20 foot lengths of #3 rebar to create a tunnel-like structure.

1. To bend rebar, two strong gardeners hold each end of the rebar and start to walk toward each other, forcing the center of the bar up into the air. It will feel a bit like you just caught a big ol' fish.

2. Walk until the ends meet each other, then push the ends deep into the ground.

3. Repeat as many times as needed, placing the bars every 4 feet or so.

4. Use wire or zip ties to fasten a horizontal piece of rebar to the top and both sides for support.

5. Now you can roll out some netting or start running twine.

These upside-down U's can also be used to create an A-frame type of structure with a scalloped top. Place two pieces side by side with the tops touching and the ends a few feet apart. Repeat, overlapping the U's to create a scalloped pattern on top. Stretch netting across the rebar and plant your beans.

Natural wood frames

If you want to work with natural wood, such as prunings, you may want to start with a more robust framework of dimensional redwood or cedar. You can achieve a very rustic look by attaching natural wood (up to a couple inches in diameter) to a structure of 2 × 2 or larger posts. Use screws or zip ties to attach the wood.

Wooden tree stakes can also make very sturdy posts and can be used in a wide variety of configurations. A very simple and efficient design is to use a stake pounder to set posts every 8 feet or so. Run wire, another post, a smaller stake, or some twine between the stakes along the top (and bottom if needed). Now roll out your netting, or start weaving twine between the horizontals.

Traditional "three sisters" method

You also have the option of going completely old school and using the traditional "three sisters" method.

1. Start by planting some grains of corn a couple of weeks before you plant your beans. Space them 8–12 inches apart.

2. When the corn sprouts are 4–6 inches tall, sow a few bean seeds around each plant.

3. Follow that in a week or two with a few winter squash seeds and sit back and watch the sisters do their thing.

Harvesting fresh Christmas Lima beans. STEVE SANDO

HARVESTING AT HOME

Harvesting your beans can be a little tedious; but it's not unpleasant if you have a friend who can help, or kids who are trying to earn more allowance. It's a great job, even for tiny, clumsy hands, and I've had some of my best conversations with my youngest son as we go down parallel rows picking pods and placing them in pillowcases.

You want to harvest the beans when the pods are dry and the beans are firm. If there's too much moisture, you can get mold on the beans and if the pods are too dry, they become brittle and the slightest touch makes them spring open and collecting the beans inside nearly impossible. In commercial fields, we measure the moisture of the plants and look to harvest at between 12 and 15 percent.

Once you've gathered up your pods, you can smash your pillowcase against the side of the house a few times or tie it up and let the kids go at it with a baseball bat, like a piñata. The pods will split open and the beans will fall to the bottom of the sack and the pods can be gently removed from the top. Don't forget to put the pods in the compost heap, or scatter them directly over your bean field.

After you've cleaned your beans, you'll see the reality of home bean gardening. It's a lot of fun and it's rewarding; but you just aren't likely to get a huge yield unless you dedicate a lot of acreage to it.

COLBY EIERMAN

Saving Seeds, Savoring Flavors

Colby Eierman is a busy man—and a popular one. A leader in sustainable gardening since his years as an undergraduate at the University of Oregon, where he founded the nonprofit School Garden Project in his senior year, Eierman is the former director of the now-legendary gardens at Napa's COPIA: The American Center for Wine, Food and the Arts. After COPIA collapsed into bankruptcy, Eierman was the director of gardens and sustainability at Benziger Family Winery before striking out on his own as an independent consultant, planning and managing private gardens around the Napa Valley. "The folks I'm growing for are a lot of homeowners and small-scale restaurants who want to harvest their own food crops," he explains. "There's so much interest right now in home food production; there's a renewed interest in stuff that tastes good."

Eierman favors heirlooms for practical reasons: "These are the varieties that have been developed to have a longer harvest season, and then also they have better flavor. They haven't been bred for some abstract concept, like the ability to be shipped well, put on a truck, or stand up to being used and abused in the marketplace; they're bred to be delicious, with a good long harvest season."

Along with his clients' gardens, Eierman also tends his own plot in south Napa. He prefers to get his seed from his own harvest or through the Seed Savers Exchange, because, he says, "the reality of the seed business is that most everything is grown overseas. If you want local seed, you're growing it yourself and you're trading it with your friends and you're a member of the Seed Savers Exchange." While saving and trading seeds may seem quaintly old-fashioned at first glance, Eierman points out that in another sense it's a very modern practice: "It's sort of a social network of vegetable growers and fruit growers and small-scale producers of food who want to preserve local varieties, and who develop and share with others. I'm trading seed with folks all over the country and beyond; it's quite a fun organization to be a part of, and as a resource for information about crops and access to cool varieties it's hard to beat." Plus, he adds, there's always the chance that your garden will sprout a genetic variation worth saving, and you'll get to put your own name on a new variety.

Beans, Eierman continues, make for an excellent introduction to seed saving because they're generally self-pollinating: "When people ask me how to get started, beans are on the list. You don't have to do a lot of work to make sure the parents are who you want them to be." They're also a breeze to grow to full maturity: "If you have a climate that allows for a long enough growing season to take a bean from sowing to actually dry, mature seeds, which is most of the U.S., it's as easy as leaving the last couple plants in a row." Horticultural-class beans, he adds, do triple duty: as young snap beans, fresh shelling beans and, finally, dried beans, with "good eating all the way through the steps."

Beans do require water; "they're not necessarily the dry farmer's choice," Eierman acknowledges. But he won't be without them: "I like to have a lot of different kinds of beans in the garden, and I'm always trying out new varieties as well."

COMMERCIAL GROWING

The process of growing beans is somewhat cumbersome for large-scale growers and they tend to grow only one or two varieties, dedicating dozens, if not hundreds, of acres to each type. The difference in yield can mean the difference between profit and loss, and commercial growers can't afford to relearn how to grow each variety every season. In addition to climate and daylight issues, the professional machinery needs to be set and calibrated differently for each variety. Most growers specialize in one bean and try and make the most of it.

Here in California, we have moderately wet winters and arid summers. Crops are watered by irrigation, and water-loving crops like corn and rice can be taxing on the system. Beans use relatively little water, and controlling the water flow via irrigation can make for a better tasting bean.

In the spring, farmers plant long rows of beans, normally two to a row, but sometimes three, depending on the variety. After the growing season ends, a tractor comes and cuts all the plants at the base and leaves them to dry further in the fields. When the plants are at their optimal moisture level (12–15 percent), they are pushed into rows by hand. Another tractor takes the big mess in the field and gently shoves it into a neat row. Now, a Rube Goldberg type machine comes along and carries pods up a conveyor belt and through chambers that break open the pods and separate the beans. The beans continue on and eventually make it over a screen that shakes wildly, removing small chaff and pebbles. The bean goes on into a holding bin, while the pods pass through a blade that sends them back into the ground as chopped green manure, improving the soil by adding natural organic matter.

The beans go through more cleaning by gravity cleaners, screens, or even sorters from an electrical eye. Most of the cleaning takes place in the field but it's that last 10 percent or so that can really make the difference. In Mexico, home cooks go through each and every bean and check for debris. Cooks in the North will check, but generally insist on a cleaner product to start with, even if it's a little more expensive. One thing everyone agrees on is that there's little worse than enjoying a gorgeous bowl of beans and biting into a small but nasty dirt clod or pebble.

50 Heirloom Beans
You Should Know

I hope you'll notice that this book isn't called *The Complete Book of Heirloom Beans* or *The Best Heirloom Beans in the World.* There are far more than 50 fabulous heirloom beans, but I wanted to focus on 50 New World varieties that I have a personal relationship with. I'd be disappointed if you stopped here with these 50 beans. While they're a good introduction to the kinds of beans, people, stories, farms, and meals I like, I hope to read about your 50 beans as well one day!

Phaseolus vulgaris Alubia Criollo

COLOR *and* MARKINGS Alubia Criollo are solid white but in a particular light, give off a hint of celadon green.

FLAVOR *and* TEXTURE When I did a TV show with Chef Emeril Lagasse, this is the bean that bowled him over. He instinctively placed the cooked beans on a bed of cooked kale and heirloom tomatoes. The chewiness of the kale and the creaminess of the beans is a great combination. Of course, other greens like mustard or chard would work well too.

Like most runner beans, you can eat them at the early stage but it's best to cook them a little longer and let them get creamy. As I said, these beans don't have a buttery flavor, but they feel indulgent in the mouth.

Alubia Criollo

*A*lubia is a difficult word in Spanish. It's fun to say. Go ahead, it's almost like singing! But it's a vague term and in Spain would mean a small to medium-sized white bean of no particular distinction. In Mexico, one of the finest beans I found was the Alubia Criollo. Criollo is like Creole; but in English, Creole would suggest something of European heritage born in the New World. In Mexico, it's the word they substitute for heirloom.

With so many white beans, you'd think they'd all be interchangeable; and for practical reasons, they are, but it's amazing how different they taste and feel. The Alubia Criollo looks a lot like the Italian Runner Cannellini, and they're both white runner beans; but the Runner Cannellinis have a buttery flavor, while the Alubias have a creamy texture but less buttery flavor. This is why collecting seeds is both fun and difficult. When rushing through a market and spying medium-sized white beans, do you stop? You do, especially if you're in a new area.

Phaseolus vulgaris Amarillo Poblano

COLOR *and* **MARKINGS** Amarillos are shaped somewhat like small limas. They curve into a "half-smile," almost like a Baby Lima and are a solid caramel yellow color.

FLAVOR *and* **TEXTURE** Amarillos have a light, nutty flavor and have more of a fudgy rather than creamy or meaty texture. They make an excellent pot bean, although the pot liquor is nothing outstanding. I like to cook them with either in a simple mirepoix (finely chopped onion, carrot, celery, garlic) and olive oil (although freshly rendered lard would be the fat of choice in Puebla), or with a ham hock or bits of pork.

Amarillo Poblano

I will always have a place in my heart for Puebla. Its role in the cuisines of Mexico reminds me of Bologna's in Italy. Both regions enjoy a rich, indulgent cuisine and they take their food very seriously. Mole poblano is clearly the most famous mole in the country and the city has an amazing collection of distinct appetizers and snacks that rival anywhere. My Puebla friends Nuria and Fernando pride themselves on knowing the best street food: which vendor makes the best pambazo or which stall has the best agua fresca. Nuria is a very patient woman and would drive me all over the state looking for heirloom beans (and new snacks). Driving around Puebla with Nuria is often spent listening to her argue with Fernando on her cell phone about where to go for the best food. These people are serious about good food.

It was with Nuria that I first decided to try importing some beans from the small producers I was meeting, instead of saving the seed growing then in the United States. She dutifully helped me find the more interesting people in the markets and we even met with State Department officials to see how they might help us with the imports.

Nuria had worked as a pastry chef for Michael Chiarello's seminal Tra Vigne restaurant in St. Helena, but obligations forced her to return to her native Puebla. I always felt guilty for dragging her here and there to help on my hunt for beans, but she told me at one point that seeing her homeland through a foreigner's eyes helped her to appreciate what she had.

Bean hunting in Puebla and nearby Cholula is easy. In the markets you see golden yellow runner beans and these lovely common beans, called simply Amarillo by the locals. The shape was a little interesting and probably what compelled me to collect them, but when I finally cooked them, I realized it was the taste that really made them worth saving.

Phaseolus vulgaris Appaloosa

COLOR *and* **MARKINGS**   Appaloosas are oval, about a half an inch in length ivory-colored, speckled with purple and mocha, not unlike Appaloosa ponies.

FLAVOR *and* **TEXTURE**   Appaloosas are best used in chili or cooked and mashed. Garnish with onions, hot peppers, and tomatoes.

Appaloosa

There are a few beans known as Appaloosa, but this one is considered the standard. Appaloosas are native to eastern Washington state and Idaho, the region that gave us the Appaloosa horse, bred by the indigenous Nez Perce tribe. It's easy to imagine one of America's most beloved horse breeds inspiring the name of this unique bean. While Appaloosas are a perfectly fine bean, their markings are the star, not the flavor. Appaloosas are similar to kidney beans, maybe a bit earthier, when cooked. As with most marked beans, the colors and patterns disappear into the pot once they've been cooked.

Both Washington state and Idaho have bean-growing traditions. Nowadays you're more likely to find commercial production of fairly typical beans like pintos, reds, pinks, and kidneys, but you can find smaller-production heirloom beans in local markets all over the Pacific Northwest. On a recent trip to Oregon, I spotted at least five variations of cranberry beans, all heirlooms and all grown from saved seed. Locals complained about shortages, and that always makes me happy. It means there's a demand, and an enterprising ag-entrepreneur can come in and take advantage of a hungry market.

I've seen cowboy cooks make up big pots of western beans using the Appaloosa. One clever cook put the beans and water and onions in an old cast iron Dutch oven and then gently laid out rashers of bacon on top from the center outwards, making almost a lid of pork. He then let it hang low and slow over a fire for the day and by dinner he had incredible beans to accompany the rest of the barbecue. I have a hunch the beans were the best part of the meal.

Phaseolus coccineus Ayocote Morado

COLOR *and* **MARKINGS** Ayocote Morado, or Purple Runners, are a solid glowing purple with an occasional darker or lighter bean.

FLAVOR *and* **TEXTURE** Runner beans tend to be big and meaty, making them incredibly versatile. Of course they work as a pot bean but I can see them in salads, soups, and even in a chili con carne. They have a slight potato starchiness about them but you can keep cooking them well beyond their "done" point as their texture goes from russet potato to creamy goodness.

Ayocote Morado

In Mexico, when I first approached my friends Gabriel and Yunuen about hunting for indigenous heirloom beans and my fantasy of importing them, they were very suspicious. From their point of view, they thought my interest in beans was a funny little quirk or eccentricity. They couldn't believe that there was a swelling interest in the United States for beans or that people were listening when I was telling them that they were a gift from Mesoamerica. Like most of us, they'd taken beans for granted. But it wasn't long until they got as excited as I am about legumes and the people who grow them.

Gabriel's mother is an excellent cook and perhaps a wee bit stubborn. She seemed to appreciate what we were doing until it came to Ayocote, or runner beans. She was of the firm opinion that they were hard to digest and caused an upset stomach. I pushed and as we collected runner beans from different growers, she tried some and confessed that they were delicious and just as easy to digest as any other bean.

In the States, we lump all runner beans together and call them scarlet runners. Almost always they're purple black with lilac spots; the scarlet refers to the flower's color, long before pods and beans are formed. Known as Ayocote Morado in Mexico, this grape-colored bean is one of the prettiest of the Ayocote varieties.

TIP If you plant any bean, I hope it's a runner bean. They germinate easily and it's a thrill to watch them grow and flower. The flowers are edible and a worthwhile addition to the garden—the pods and later beans are an added treat.

Phaseolus coccineus Ayocote Negro

COLOR *and* **MARKINGS** Ayocote Negro is solid black, with maybe a few stray dark purples mixed in. The large size and slightly oblong shape makes them easy to identify.

FLAVOR *and* **TEXTURE** Black runners are very much like their purple brothers, Ayocote Morado. In fact, you could use them interchangeably. They tend to be a little starchier than the lighter-colored runner beans, but not unpleasantly so. They make the perfect salad bean and their earthiness makes them an ideal match for sautéed wild mushrooms with loads of garlic.

Ayocote Negro

On the surface, the Ayocote Negro is just another runner bean, this time black. But one of my favorite tricks is to show a bag of the beans in their cello packaging, cut it open and then pour the beans into a bowl. I'm not exaggerating when I say that almost everyone gasps at how pretty these black beans are. They look like beautiful little pebbles and the compulsion to touch them is overwhelming.

In Mexico, you see runner beans (Ayocote) all over the markets but rarely, if ever, in a restaurant. They take a little longer to cook and they're different from common beans. It's a shame they're so neglected even in their native homeland. You can eat them at all stages, but normally you cook them either as fresh shelled beans or dried.

It's important to note that even though these are beans and they're black, they don't necessarily make a good substitute for black (or turtle) beans. Normally when someone refers to a black bean in a recipe, they are referring to a common bean (*Phaseolus vulgaris*), such as the Midnight bean, not a runner (*P. coccineus*).

Black beans have a distinct flavor and inky black pot liquor. Ayocote is starchier and the bean can be three times as big as a traditional black bean.

Phaseolus lunatus Baby Lima

COLOR *and* MARKINGS Mostly you see Baby Limas, even the heirloom varieties, in white. In the Yucatan and other parts of Mayan Mexico, Baby Limas are called Balero Teopiscas and are smaller and red. They generally grow in pods that are half-moon shaped, looking like lop-sided smiles. The beans, both Baby Limas and larger ones, have a distinctive pudgy shape.

FLAVOR *and* TEXTURE If you grew up hating limas as I did, you really owe it to yourself to grab a bag and see if your disdain for them may have had more to do with your mother's cooking skills than the beans themselves, especially the dried ones. I've come to love their starchy texture and good pot liquor. Because they are mild, they work well with bacon or butter or as an ingredient in a more complex dish, like a traditional southern succotash. They don't make a good pot bean, but they definitely deserve our attention.

Baby Lima

I often say if my point of reference with beans were canned red kidneys, I'd probably hate beans as well. I was lucky enough to grow up in the San Francisco Bay Area where a lot of different cultures met up to expose me to beans. Dinners in North Beach meant Borlotti beans and pasta, and taco night at home always included a large can of Rosarita brand refried beans that my father would "doctor up." Car trips down I-5 would include some famous pea soup; and my interest in things Indian led me to a small but determined Indian population, who introduced me to curries and legumes that I had never imagined. The one negative bean experience I had was shared with millions of other children across the nation and that was the frozen "vegetable medley" served at home, and in restaurants and cafeterias across the country. Cubed carrots, cubed potatoes, and small, Baby Limas were tossed with margarine and then the adults would wonder why we hated vegetables, lima beans in particular.

Meeting up with Baby Limas years later, I've come to the pleasant surprise that they're very good. Often they are called butter beans, but not because they're buttery. No, you need to add butter to them. I've met some Southerners who insist that only Baby Limas, and not the large ones, are to be called butter beans. I'll stick to Baby Limas if it's that much of a problem!

TIP Limas have a built-in toxin that disappears when cooking, so you need to cook them for a portion of the time without a lid to allow the toxin to escape. Normally this isn't a problem; I've never heard of anyone actually getting sick from eating limas that were cooked covered. If you have a good bean pot, you really only use the lid while the beans are coming up to their initial boil and then only add the lid if you need to build up the heat. If you should decide to make limas in a slow cooker, I'd err on the side of caution and remove the lid for the last hour of cooking.

Phaseolus lunatus Balero Teopisca

COLOR *and* **MARKINGS**   Balero Teopiscas are Baby Limas with their familiar "smile" shape. They have a gorgeous tomato red color that changes to brick red soon after harvest.

FLAVOR *and* **TEXTURE**   Balero Teopiscas are virtually identical to Baby Limas. They have a more vegetable flavor than other beans but can be used anywhere Baby Limas or butter beans are called for. Because of their small size, they're quick cooking.

Balero Teopisca

Wanting to try all avenues for seed saving and finding new sources, I went to a very large trade show in Guadalajara. The real customers were there to fill their market shelves with innovative products from all over Mexico. I had a feeling I'd find some bean growers that would have some connections to heirlooms. I was told that it would take days to make my way through the convention hall, but when I arrived, I saw it was not going to be the goldmine I'd hoped for. Women in miniskirts dancing to loud music urged passersby to sample their Red Bull energy drinks made me shake my head and wonder what any of this had to do with food!

I quickly discovered the commercial booths were going to lead me nowhere fast, but the booths that represented the agricultural departments of the various states might prove more fruitful. From the Oaxacan government, I was given a big swig of mescal and the promise of all the cooperation I needed in the future. From Sonora, I was promised names of farmers who still grew heritage varieties; and best of all, from Chiapas, I was given a kilo of Balero Teopiscas, their red Baby Limas.

When I got home, I grew them in my trial gardens in Napa and they were slow to germinate and flower, but once they got going (and summer was in high gear), they wouldn't quit and kept producing until late fall.

Phaseolus vulgaris Bayo Coquin

COLOR *and* MARKINGS Bayo Coquins are cream-colored beans with mottled marks in pink and purple; they enjoy the same basic colors as Flor de Mayo and Flor de Junio, perhaps a little darker.

FLAVOR *and* TEXTURE Bayo Coquins have a full bodied, beany flavor and rich, almost fudge-like texture.

Bayo Coquin

Bayo Coquin is a pretty bean with the same color palette as Flor de Mayo and Flor de Junio. I think of it as their slightly savage first cousin. I've only seen them grown on a very small scale and always as a pole bean. Despite their thick skin, they're prized in Mexico as a refried filling for tlacoyos, a torpedo-shaped corn masa appetizer. The filling is easy enough to make and shouldn't be limited to tlacoyos, so it's in your best interest to find your favorite bean spread. Traditional Mexican cooks fry white onions in rich, hot lard until the onions are translucent and then add some cooked beans and broth, mashing the whole mess with a potato masher, or even better, a wooden machacadora, designed specifically to mash beans. If this is too rich for your everyday life, you can also just take some beans, their broth, and half an onion and blend it in a blender until smooth and then heat up this paste in a pan. It's not as rich and indulgent, but it's perfectly delicious and an ideal food to slather over hot tortillas or other masa treats. As much as I love Mexican lard, I do have to admit the cooked beans last much longer in the refrigerator if made with olive oil instead of my beloved manteca.

Traditionally Bayo Coquins were cracked in a metate, a traditional lava stone mortar that has been largely replaced by the electric blender, then cooked with chile and cumin to make a paste used in tlacoyos or gorditas de frijol. Many, many pots later, I can tell you the traditional way of cooking them in a pot, with a few aromatics, is also excellent!

Phaseolus vulgaris Black Pinto

COLOR *and* **MARKINGS** The markings are the same mottled "paint" look you see on a traditional pinto but the colors are tan and a dark, fountain pen–ink-black. Once cooked, they look like traditional pintos.

FLAVOR *and* **TEXTURE** The flavor is much like an ordinary pinto. The real interest is in the raw, dried look. But don't shortchange the lowly pinto! It's an incredibly popular bean for a good reason. Pintos are versatile and delicious.

Black Pinto

The intention of the organization Native Seeds/SEARCH may be to preserve the food plants of Northern Mexico and the American Southwest, but anyone with a passing interest in gardening from seed will enjoy the work they're doing and look forward to their seed catalog each winter. In particular, people living in deserts or drought conditions will appreciate their seed saving and data collection for growing in arid climates. I first learned about tepary beans from them. They also have different varieties of tomatillos, tomatoes, and of course, chiles.

One of my favorites beans of theirs to grow at home has been the Black Pinto. It's easy to grow, and if you do some seed saving, you'll have your own seed stock before long. It's also incredibly pretty.

Visit Native Seeds/SEARCH at www.nativeseeds.org or at their retail store and headquarters in Tucson, Arizona.

Phaseolus acutifolius Blue Speckled Tepary

COLOR *and* **MARKINGS**   A quick glance might make you think these beans are solid blue, but if you look closely, you'll see they are tan with purple-blue veins running across them. The beans are small, and less agile eyes might need a little microscopic help to really appreciate how pretty they are.

FLAVOR *and* **TEXTURE**   Blue Speckled Teparies are like other tepary varieties. I find them a little mealy and less sweet than a White Tepary, which works better for savory cooking.

Blue Speckled Tepary

I have two wonderful sons, Nico and Robby, and I've always wanted them to have at least a casual interest in gardening and farming. I know from my own experience that you can only push so hard before young people push back. I decided a quiet example would be the best path for success.

My younger son, Nico, took to the mud like a duck to water. Robby, the oldest, was a little tougher. One season, we planted rows of corn with beans between the corn stalks. Beans are fine and quick but corn is so impressive, it's hard not to be swept up in the drama of nature. They start as blades of grass and quickly turn to poles, followed by the tassels and actual ears of corn. Plus, when you grow organically, you have lots of treats, in the form of worms for the chickens, hiding in the beautiful ripe ears. Robby was finally enchanted and the plot was beautiful. Corn takes a lot more water than tepary beans need, so we had lots of pretty flowers and foliage but not a huge yield of beans, but it didn't seem to matter. One late summer afternoon, after a Sunday of work, I said to my son, "Look what we did! We made this happen! We put the seeds in the ground, we watered, we took care of them, and now we have a corn and bean field! We did this!"

I was on my knees pointing and Robby put his arms around my shoulders and said, "We sure like farming, don't we Papa?"

Of course I melted and the plot of corn and Blue Speckled Tepary beans have become a tradition. I couldn't stop him from playing video games, but I am happy that he's more well rounded.

TIP   Once they are established and flowers are blooming, it's a good idea to stress the plants a bit by holding back the water to increase your yield. This makes them less than ideal for planting with corn, but sometimes high yield isn't a priority!

Phaseolus vulgaris Borlotti

COLOR *and* MARKINGS Most Borlotti beans have a tan background and spotted stripes in a contrasting color, often blood-red or black. Once cooked, they become brown all the way through.

FLAVOR *and* TEXTURE Despite looking a little bit like elaborate pintos, Borlottis have a much different texture. Their skin is a little thicker and the meat of the bean is velvety as opposed to creamy. Despite their thicker skins, they exude an indulgent bean broth, which is why so many versions of Italian pasta e fagioli (or pasta fazool) use Borlottis.

Borlotti

Borlottis are cranberry beans. There are dozens of varieties; and even within Italy, you won't find two communities that can agree on what makes a Borlotti. My friend Eileen has a strong Italian background and would often travel to Italy to see her not-so-distant cousins. She remembers a particular bean as Borlotti and has spent many years trying to track it down. The closest thing she has found is a cranberry from Colombia, and it's not quite the right bean.

There's a classic soup from Pátzcuaro, Michoacán, that is basically one part tomatoes, one part chicken stock, and one part pureed beans. The bean they like is a mild, almost bland, Bayo bean. I once used Borlottis by accident and I think the soup was superior. Since then, I always consider this as the basis for a great soup. Of course, other beans would probably be great too, but the velvety texture of the Borlotti is easy to like.

Phaseolus acutifolius Brown Tepary

COLOR *and* MARKINGS Brown Teparies are solid, small beans that look a lot like lentils. There are dozens, if not hundreds of varieties of tepary, some solid, and some with markings or multicolors.

FLAVOR *and* TEXTURE Brown Tepary beans have just a hint of sweetness, while the white variety can be almost cloyingly sweet. When fully cooked, they have a meatiness and denseness that's not off-putting, but they're not as indulgent-tasting as other beans.

Brown Tepary

I can't think of a bean that better represents the need to protect our heirloom varieties than the Brown Tepary. Native to Northern Mexico and the American Southwest, teparies are higher in protein and fiber than other beans, which are super foods in their own right. Native Americans have bred the bean to be drought tolerant, so it can grow almost anywhere there's a need for a cheap, filling, and healthy protein. To top it all off, it has a great flavor and is incredibly versatile in the kitchen.

Currently in Mexico teparies remain popular only in the extreme north. Here in the States, the beans have experienced a revival, thanks in good part to the O'odham Indian tribe. In California, tepary beans have been grown since at least 1900. The summer droughts and quick-growing nature of tepary beans make a perfect match.

Phaseolus vulgaris Caballero

COLOR *and* **MARKINGS**   Caballeros are small, white, and round with no distinguishing marks.

FLAVOR *and* **TEXTURE**   The beans are very mild, allowing the aromatic vegetables to shine. The bean broth is rich and the texture of the beans is like heavy cream.

Caballero

After growing our beans in Northern California for years, I longed to meet bean growers in Latin America and build relationships with them. My fantasy was to one day be able to import beans under the Rancho Gordo name and encourage smaller farmers to continue to grow their heritage beans as they had for generations, instead of raising bland hybrids that seemed destined for a post-NAFTA international market. There's nothing wrong with producing a lot of beans, bland or not, to feed a lot of people, but the smaller farmers tend to get lost in the shuffle without the big promotions and subsidies that bigger commercial growers enjoy. I'm on board for good, cheap food; but I think preserving our agrarian heritage is equally important, not just for genetic diversity but also for flavor and keeping the spirit of the small farmer alive.

I've gone on to develop relationships with growers in Mexico and I was pretty excited to receive a call from Betsy and Marion from Culinary Collective in the Pacific Northwest. They were in Peru and met some bean growers and thought of me. They were going to send me some samples of their beans and I was thrilled, even though I would have loved to hop on a plane and join them in Peru instead. I love traveling and the thought of seeing the Incan ruins and feeling the acidic juice from some cool ceviche run down my chin entered my mind. Still, the big issue was finding great beans and encouraging their growth through sales. Cold beers in a ceviche shack would have to wait.

When the beans arrived, I first grabbed for the bag marked Caballero (rider or horseman) for no particular reason. As was the norm, I cooked them in a simple mirepoix with good olive oil, nothing more. I had some good friends over for beers and dominoes, and at one point we stopped to taste the new beans. There was a dead silence until I said, "This is why I do what I do. These are incredible." My guests grabbed spoons and bowls and tasting went to consumption and a new favorite bean was discovered.

Phaseolus vulgaris California

COLOR *and* **MARKINGS** California beans are a solid, almost gunmetal gray with no markings. When very fresh, they have a slight violet hue.

FLAVOR *and* **TEXTURE** California beans are dense and meaty. You could substitute Santa Maria Pinquitos and I doubt you'd know the difference when cooked, which makes them an ideal chili bean as well.

California

The Seed Savers Exchange is a great organization for buying heirloom seeds to grow in your own garden. Once you get the hang of it, it feels like something is missing when you buy vegetable starts at the nursery or even order seeds from a commercial catalog. Saving seeds and sharing your bounty is up there with roller coaster rides and trips to Europe, in my mind. Nothing is quite as satisfying as meeting up with a fellow gardener who is sincerely happy that you're sharing your seeds. Eating the bounty and breaking bread at the end of the season is a pretty fine thing, as well.

You can share seeds with your neighbors, fellow Master Gardeners, or the kids at school, but you can also list them in the annual Seed Savers Exchange book and share them with other seed savers, and request some of your own. No money is made, but shipping costs are covered and you receive an annual yearbook that lists all the seeds and varieties available. It's like a gardener's dream to browse the big book, which is where I first encountered California beans. I was a little disappointed when the bean arrived. They were a blah gray color with the subtlest hint of purple. I was more interested in the exotic markings than anything else at that point, but I dutifully planted them and waited to see what happened. It turns out my Napa climate was ideal and as these things grew, I understood the genesis of the Jack and the Beanstalk fable. While the other beans were struggling to get established, the Californias were thriving and even blossoming. The leaves were large and beautiful and when it came time to pod, there were dozens and dozens.

Phaseolus vulgaris Cargamanto Colombiano

COLOR *and* MARKINGS The red Cargamanto bean is really a gorgeous specimen. The red-chocolate background is a beautiful base for little yellow specks.

FLAVOR *and* TEXTURE Like all cranberry beans, Cargamantos have a luxurious feel in the mouth, as if you are eating something incredibly indulgent and fattening. The bean itself is velvety and the pot liquor is thick and rich, made even more so if you smash a ladleful up and then return them to the pot.

Cargamanto Colombiano

haven't had the chance to visit Colombia yet, but I feel very close to this country. The music makes my hips sway in a rather carefree manner and their love of beans makes it a wise country. My friends Jane and John King founded a great organization called Friends of Colombian Orphans (www.friendsofcolombianorphans.org) that helps train girls in trades that they can use throughout their lives. The Kings spent a lot of time in Colombia arranging to adopt their wonderful daughter Nataly and would regularly post photos from their journeys. Of course it was nice to see the fried treats, the churches, the markets, the arepas, and the countryside, but it was a stray photo of a bowl of the most delicious-looking beans that rocked my world. They were soupy brown beans with a wandering piece of pork or two floating around. In one sense, this could have been almost any Latin American country, but this plate of beans had me going.

I've since discovered the Cargamanto bean. It's beautiful when raw, and rich and soupy when cooked. It's related to the cranberry bean, so you can always substitute cranberries, Borlotti, or Tongues of Fire. There are also white Cargamantos (which are pretty much like our cranberry beans), but these red Cargamantos are standard. Just looking at them you can begin to understand how delicious and rich they are, if that's possible!

Phaseolus lunatus Christmas Lima

COLOR *and* MARKINGS Christmas Limas have a brick red color and milky cream markings, both of which darken as the bean ages. Personally, I think they're one of the prettiest and most unusual looking beans out there.

FLAVOR *and* TEXTURE As noted, there's a slightly grainy, chestnut-like texture to the bean; but if you cook them long enough, they end up being creamy. They can take a lot of abuse in the kitchen, so be sure to include them in dishes that benefit from long, slow cooking times. Their pot liquor is rich and deep, almost beefy. Of course you could use them in soups, salads, and as a vegetable side dish; and unlike their cousins, the Baby Limas, I think they make a fine pot bean.

Christmas Lima

I hate lima beans!" is the reaction I get from most people when I show them the otherwise appealing Christmas Lima. I was sure I hated them, too. I also hated beets and anchovies, but once I actually tasted all of these things cooked properly, they made sense and became a part of my diet.

I think what people believe they don't like is actually a Baby Lima, fresh or frozen. These vegetables are pretty starchy and they taste like a vegetable, not a bean. There isn't that indulgent creaminess or savory punch you get from a Borlotti or a pinto. Remembering the taste of a frozen Baby Lima and seeing the mammoth size of the Christmas Lima, I can understand why the reaction might be less than positive.

Luckily, I'm persuasive and most people hate to miss out on a good thing so they try them. And then they come back. Often they'll tell me this is their new favorite bean and I can only nod in agreement. It's tremendous!

Here in the States, this monster is known as the Christmas Lima, and, occasionally, the Chestnut Lima. It has a distinct chestnut texture and possibly taste, but the taste is so subtle it's up for debate. In Italy, the Christmas Lima is known as Fagiolo di Papa, or the Pope's bean. Its roots probably lie in Peru.

You don't see it grown commercially often, but almost all the seed catalogs have Christmas Limas for growing at home. If you have a short season, you can eat them as a shelling bean.

TIP Again, this shouldn't be a problem, but limas supposedly have a toxic element to them that cooks off. Because of this, you should be sure to cook the beans with the lid mostly off. I'm not really sure if this is true or an old wives' tale, but I think it's better to err on the side of prevention, especially since you'll be doing this anyway except in very rare cases.

Phaseolus vulgaris Classic Cranberry

COLOR *and* MARKINGS The colors can change, but tan and pink or pinky-browns are the norm. The markings look like disturbed swirls of some kind.

FLAVOR *and* TEXTURE These beans have been popular for a reason. They have a nice, almost nutty flavor and a smooth texture. Some have very thin skins, which would make you think of them as a good candidate for refried beans, but there's something weird about refried cranberry beans. It just doesn't work. The thin skins do mean a good release of pot liquor, hence their popularity in dishes like pasta e fagioli where the liquid coats each noodle. Also consider them with grains where the luxurious liquid coats each grain.

Classic Cranberry

The term "cranberry bean" covers a big group of beans that all enjoy similar markings and lots of different colorations. Originating in Colombia, the cranberry traveled from there, and travel it did. In Italy, many of the Borlotti beans are varieties of the classic cranberry. Spain's Toloso bean is thought to be a descendant as well. I was in Lucca and found their special red bean, but a closer inspection revealed it as yet another variation of this good bean. In Mexico, you'll find cranberries known as Cacahuate, or peanut, beans.

Phaseolus vulgaris Coconita (Coton del Indio)

COLOR *and* **MARKINGS**   We might take the pinto for granted, but look closely and take note of how beautiful they can be! Fresh Coconitos have a pink background and tannish markings.

FLAVOR *and* **TEXTURE**   Pintos, Coconitos, and all their cousins seem to produce a superior pot liquor and solid, good beans. They are versatile enough to use in anything from pot beans to pinto bean pie.

Coconita (Coton del Indio)

When my friends Gabriel and Yunuen showed me this bean they had found in the wonderful market at Ixmiquilpan, I said, "It's just a pinto!" They looked at me like I was a little nuts. Being from Hidalgo and Mexico City, respectively, they had had little exposure to what we call a common pinto bean. To them this was soft, exotic, and romantic. I cooked it and it was excellent, but it definitely was what we know of as a pinto.

When the Coconita comes straight out of the fields, the markings are a lot softer and prettier, and the colors are pink and tan. There are darker versions of pintos, like Rattlesnake beans, but in general, you can tell the freshness by the color.

Phaseolus vulgaris Deer's Eye (Ojo de Venado)

COLOR *and* **MARKINGS** Ojo de Venados have a mottled tan and cream-colored body. The "eye" is surrounded by distinctive darker brown markings.

FLAVOR *and* **TEXTURE** Deer's Eye beans are very meaty and have the dense, grainy texture of a tepary bean. The pot liquor is thin and brown, but flavorful. I've had them mostly as a simple pot bean and in chili con carne.

Deer's Eye (Ojo de Venado)

For vacations, most of my friends like to go to Europe and visit the masters or fly down to Mexico and relax in the sun. I admit, there's nothing quite so wonderful as bodysurfing and sunbathing on a Mexican beach and having someone bring you cold beers and ceviche. I used to be able to relax like this for a week solid, but now I grow antsy and impatient, wondering if there isn't a market nearby and is it possible there might be an heirloom bean to discover. Most communities have a permanent market structure and these are fine, but the real fun for me is at a tianguis, which is usually an open air market that seems thrown together, normally in the same place one day a week. A tianguis, like markets, is often divided up loosely by sections and the bean sellers are often together. Sometimes several sellers will have the same beans, and I always find this suspicious. It may mean the bean is popular and several farmers grow it, but it most likely means they aren't really growers and they all got it from the same source. On the outskirts of markets you will often find indigenous farmers who sell on grass mats and have one or two neat piles of beans in front of them. This is where I find the really rare beans that you just don't see every day. Unfortunately, sometimes it's the last time you'll see the bean unless you grab it.

Deer's Eye was found on the edge of the market on grass mats. I thought it was rather uninteresting until I noticed the markings around the "eye" of the bean. It's a relatively unknown bean that grows in Durango, Guanajuato, Zacatecas, and north of San Luis Potosí. It is not a bean in fashion for many growers—you'd be lucky to find one grower with more than 50 kilos at a typical market. It is really an heirloom bean of the North and the Bajío.

Phaseolus vulgaris Eye of the Goat

COLOR *and* MARKINGS Eye of the Goat really look somewhat like goat's eyes. Tan beans with brown stripes cover a medium-sized bean.

FLAVOR *and* TEXTURE I love the way these beans just melt in your mouth, even though they do have a little texture. It's soft and pillowy, not starchy or dense. The liquid that surrounds each bean is thick and dense without being overpowering. This is an ideal pot bean. While it needs nothing more, I always appreciate a little fresh, minced onion for texture and if I've used a lot of olive oil (or lard) a little lime juice is nice, but not mandatory.

Eye of the Goat

At the farmers markets, people will ask, "What's your favorite bean?" and I counter with, "Which is your favorite child?" If I haven't been punched in the nose, I tell them I can't say one bean is The Best. I love them all, but in different ways and in different dishes. I can say that I have some all-around favorites for my way of cooking, and Eye of the Goat is on the top of the list. They look interesting enough, like actual goat's eyes; but then you cook them, preferably with just onion, garlic, olive oil, water, and salt and then the heavens open up, the angels sing, and you float among the clouds, filled with hope and beans.

I must sound boring and strident when I strongly suggest cooking the beans simply in order to really enjoy what makes them so special. "Oh, I agree! I just cook them with a ham hock!" many people respond. Now, I love beans and pork but I promise you, you've missed what makes this bean so good when you cook it with a ham hock. Suddenly it's a pork dish, not a bean dish. It won't be bad, and in fact it might be great, but you won't understand the glory of heirloom beans until you let them stand on their own.

Phaseolus vulgaris Eye of the Tiger (Ojo de Tigre)

COLOR *and* **MARKINGS** With the coloring of a tiger and the common "eye" pattern, these are easily one of the most visually beautiful beans collected.

FLAVOR *and* **TEXTURE** Unfortunately, Tiger Eyes tend to fall apart easily, but this only means they work better as a refried bean or a soup bean. They're also worthy of pasta e fagioli, with the rich liquid coating each noodle.

Eye of the Tiger (Ojo de Tigre)

It's easy to fall in love with Tiger Eyes, also known as Pepa de Zapallo. They have a rich orange and brown color that just looks like it's going to be delicious, and of course it is. Originating in Argentina or possibly Chile, they remain popular in pockets of Italy, but I've only encountered them from other heirloom growers and home seed savers, and in stories from travelers to Argentina.

Most beans can be eaten during one of the many stages of growth with varying degrees of success. You can eat the flowers, you can eat the pods (but don't forget to de-string them!), you can shell them when fully developed, or of course you can leave them to dry. Tiger Eyes have very thin skins, which means they'll fall apart after so much cooking. This is a blessing if you're making soups or refried beans. It's somewhat of a drag of you're making cassoulet or a bean salad. But this same thin skin makes Eye of the Tiger an excellent, smallish, shelling bean. If you grow some, you can try for yourself. After shelling, just cook them for about 35 minutes in boiling water and toss with butter and olive oil.

Phaseolus vulgaris Flageolet

COLOR *and* **MARKINGS** Flageolets are mostly mint green, with some of the beans white. They would be all green if the grower could manage to get the field to ripen at the same time but, it's next to impossible. White in the mix isn't an indication of quality. They cook up to a light tan.

FLAVOR *and* **TEXTURE** There was a time I would have declared Flageolet as bland and uninteresting, but "mild" is a better word. "Perfect companion" is an even better description. The beans have a natural affinity to lamb and fish, but I love the creaminess of the beans when mixed with roasted tomatoes and garlic: a perfect side dish for any grilled meat.

Flageolet

When I first started getting obsessed with beans, I tended to discount Flageo-let. In part, this was a reaction to the ridiculous response from Francophiles who seemed to swoon when they saw we were growing them. They would ignore all the other beans and focus on what I perceived as a bland, lackluster legume compared to the more exciting beans like Christmas Limas and scarlet runners. To be honest, I felt like these people only liked the Flageolet because they were French and if, say, Baby Limas were popular in France, this would have been their bean instead. I was wrong about Flageolet and there's a good chance I'm wrong about Francophiles as well, but I doubt it.

The funny thing is that some bean historians trace the origin of Flageolets to Oaxaca, Mexico. Vive la différence!

Flageolets will stay whole and not fall apart, even after a lot of cooking, which is why a lot of chefs use them in cassoulet instead of the more authentic, but rare and shockingly expensive, Tarbais bean. Kate Hill, an American living in Camont, France—real cassoulet country—says locals use Tarbais (from nearby Tarbes), but also lentils, coco blanc, and coco noir. Kate loves cooking most any bean, but Flageolet in particular, tossed in glorious duck fat.

TIPS Because Flageolets are so good at remaining whole, you may want to take a cup of the beans from the pot, mash them with a bean masher, potato masher, or immersion blender, and then return them to the pot when making a creamy soup.

Because of their mild flavor, Flageolets are the perfect showcase for an array of herbs. You could make a mix of your favorite, or as I prefer, pick a single herb, like thyme, and just show it off on its own.

Phaseolus vulgaris Flor de Junio

COLOR *and* **MARKINGS** Flor de Junio have beautiful lilac and yellow cream colors , and their markings are exotic swirls, like a 1960s silk scarf. Like the Flor de Mayo (and Rosa de Castilla), these beans don't age well and the subtle colors turn to browns and tans.

FLAVOR *and* **TEXTURE** There's little difference between the Flor beans but they all share a delicate, light body that welcomes pork, mirepoix, or other flavorings. They tend to be neutral and light, yet they keep their shape while cooking and almost melt in your mouth once you start eating.

Flor de Junio

Michoacán is a remarkable state in Mexico, but a lot of us don't know much about it because there aren't any great, easy-to-reach resorts there. It's a shame because culturally and culinarily, it's a marvel! And if you live in northern California, there's a good chance your Mexican neighbor has roots in this state. If you are lucky enough to be invited to share a meal, chances are the bean of choice is going to be Flor de Mayo or Flor de Junio.

TIP A friend in Patzcuaro, in the heart of Michoacán, likes to cook a piece of bacon and then remove it, saving the fat for frying onions and garlic, making the vegetables and lard the basis for seasoning her beans. At the end she crumbles some queso fresco over each dish and little chopped up bits of the original piece of bacon.

Phaseolus lunatus Florida Butter

COLOR *and* **MARKINGS** The beans are very white with sharp black markings when young. As they age, the white becomes creamier and the black a little duller. They turn brown when fully cooked.

FLAVOR *and* **TEXTURE** Like all limas, especially the baby varieties, they can be dense and creamy but they enjoy a more "vegetable-like" taste than regular beans.

Florida Butter

realize that even though my goal is to create a thriving company that earns enough to support my growing travel habit, part of what I do is public service, especially at the farmers market or our retail store. Some of our customers have come to buy beans. Others, often seniors, are passing the time and that's fine with me. They'll look at all the beans and laugh and remember how they had to endure beans during leaner years. Often they'll stop for a moment, reflect, then lean in and ask me if I've come across this or that bean. If this senior is a southerner, more often it's the Florida Butter bean that makes them nostalgic.

It was after tasting the Florida Butter bean that I became brave enough to try other lima beans. They weren't the overly starchy, chewy wads I was expecting. They were light and good! It turns out they are very popular in the South, in part because they can tolerate and even thrive in a hot and humid climate. I was recently in Chiapas, in Mexico, almost on the Guatemalan border, and among the very distinct, unusual beans of the region, I found Florida Butter beans. I'm sure they started out in Meso America and made their way up to Florida, but it was a real kick in the pants to find this obscure bean thriving in Mexico.

Also known as Calico beans, Calico Pole beans, or Florida Speckled Limas, Florida Butter beans are a Baby Lima that in my mind are best used as an ingredient in a more elaborate dish, but I've met many Southerners who like nothing more than a bowl full of speckled limas smothered in butter with salt.

Phaseolus vulgaris Good Mother Stallard

COLOR *and* MARKINGS Good Mother Stallards are purple with really odd and wonderful cream-colored spots, lines, and flecks. Some of the beans have more cream than others and they look like some kind of mish-mash of pintos, cranberries, and the Milky Way at dusk. There's really no other bean quite like them.

FLAVOR *and* TEXTURE Some beans are creamy, some beans are velvety and Good Mother Stallards are silky. They have fairly tough skins but they break easily and release one of the best, if not the best, pot liquors of any bean I know.

I've had Good Mother Stallards that were grown in Holland but they were anemic and light compared to the ones I've had grown domestically. I suspect it was more an issue of terroir than genetics or sloppy farming.

Good Mother Stallard

For an all-around great bean that showcases why we bother with heirloom varieties and seed saving, I can't think of a better candidate than Good Mother Stallard. This bean, with just a little olive oil, onion, garlic, salt, and water, almost always knocks the socks off the lucky eater. I don't think there's a better all-around pot bean out there, yet Good Mother Stallards are mild enough to be used in other recipes as well.

Good Mother Stallards are incredibly versatile. They make an excellent pot bean so by all means, go ahead and enjoy a bowlful on their own. I've made a great dish of fresh chanterelle mushrooms, sautéed at a high heat, with garlic and dried oregano, tossed with cooked Good Mother Stallards. The flavor was woodsy and wintery and indulgent. I've also made excellent charro beans with bacon, tomatoes, and chiles. I can imagine them working in almost any cuisine.

Phaseolus vulgaris Hidatsa Red

COLOR *and* **MARKINGS** Hidatsa Reds are solid round beans with no markings. The beans are a slightly oval shape and are medium-sized.

FLAVOR *and* **TEXTURE** For me, the real thrill of the red beans is their pot liquor. Whether tossed with some steaming hot quinoa, brown rice, or noodles, the bean broth is like a soup or even a sauce. The beans are plump and brown when cooked. I've heard some chefs say they insist on pork with red beans and while I agree it's excellent, it's a little silly. Vegetarian red beans are fine as well.

Hidatsa Red

I love almost all of the red beans, except maybe kidneys, which I think are just a little boring. The variations among the different heirloom types aren't as distinct as for pintos, blacks, or other common beans, but it's important that gardeners and farmers keep growing them. They're our edible history and it would be a shame if we lost this key part of who we are.

The Hidatsa tribe of Native Americans is from the Dakotas. The Oscar Will Seed Company got their original stock of red beans from the Hidatsa people and offered them in their catalog in the late 1800s, making it popular among gardeners all over the country. Hidatsa Reds have since fallen out of favor, but a big push by the Seed Savers Exchange seems to have made them commercially viable again. I've found them very difficult to grow, but there's a good chance my seed stock was the problem.

Phaseolus vulgaris Lila

COLOR *and* MARKINGS Lilas are lilac-colored and round with no markings, although the color has a gradual variance from light to dark on some beans.

FLAVOR *and* TEXTURE Lilas are light and easy to pair with other foods. They shine on their own as a pot bean, but benefit from a little pork if you have it. They have a good pot liquor so consider them for rice dishes and pasta e fagioli. Lila's are also known as Appetito, and one taste helps you to understand why.

Lila

Lila was one of the first beans we started to import with the Rancho Gordo-Xoxoc Project. In the past, I'd go to markets, buy some interesting beans, trial them in my Napa gardens, and see what happened. Then I met Gabriel and Yunuen, who make treats from their local sour prickly pear plants (xoconostle, pronounced "cho-co-no-s-tle") and sell them under the company name Xoxoc, through Mexico City food diva Ruth Alegria. Together, Gabriel, Yunuen, and I have met with small producers and have arranged to buy their harvests of heirloom beans. When I would attempt to do this alone, I was met with a lot of resistance. Traditionally, in encounters with gringos from up north, Mexicans, especially the indigenous people, don't tend to come out on the winning end of the stick. From their perspective, they couldn't figure out why I was interested in their beans. Heirloom varieties were losing ground in Mexico, why on earth should there be a market in the United States? Gabriel and Yunuen, both Mexican, are incredibly patient and understanding in a way I am not.

After a lot of relationship building and, thankfully, good meals including beans and homemade tortillas, we finally imported the heirloom beans into the United States without much trouble. The farmers were thrilled that they didn't have to take the beans to market, so all the risk about sales vanished. They were also able to continue to grow their heritage varieties as they have for hundreds of years, instead of falling under the pressure to grow bland hybrids, like Michigan Blacks. Some farmers who stop growing their own beans and grow more commercial varieties find the Chinese and Americans have undersold them by the time they bring them to market, making their crops worth less and less. In 2009, the last protections for Mexican bean and corn production were dropped under NAFTA and now it's going to be a challenge to encourage Mexicans to continue to produce heirloom varieties. Creating new markets, such as here in the States, is one tactic that seems to be working.

Phaseolus vulgaris Mantequilla

COLOR *and* **MARKINGS** Small round beans with no markings and a butter-cream color.

FLAVOR *and* **TEXTURE** Mantequilla do not have an exquisite pot liquor, but they are a nice dense little bean.

Mantequilla

There are numerous beans called Mantequilla (or butter) beans. American butter beans are, of course, Baby Limas. I've seen some Baby Limas in Mexico marked as Mantequilla, but normally it's a different bean altogether. I found some delicious examples in Guanajuato while on a tour with food historian Rachel Laudan, who was patient with me as I scoured the countryside looking for new beans and bean pots. The Mantequilla beans were small and round and only resembled butter in color. When I cooked them, they were nice and meaty, almost like a white chili bean.

I've tried to grow them here in California, but I'm afraid they'll have to remain a Mexican treat. Either the climate or the number of daylight hours made them not feel welcome in my trial gardens. This actually happens more often than I care to admit. I'll collect beans from a good source and they'll germinate beautifully and send up plants that grow and grow until you're convinced you can climb up the beanstalks and meet Jack and his giant. But no flowers! And without flowers, we have no pods and of course no beans. I've tried cutting back the water and stressing the plants, and I've tried extra TLC, even singing show tunes in the fields in order to coax blooms, but if it's not meant to be, it's not meant be, so Mantequilla, among others, won't be a California bean.

Phaseolus vulgaris Moro

COLOR *and* MARKINGS Moro's colors obviously reminded someone of the Moors in Spain. The small beans have swirling gray or brown backgrounds and black mottled markings and the eyes are dramatically circled in black.

FLAVOR *and* TEXTURE Moros are excellent beans, but their looks are what make them distinctive. They have a nice, generic beanFlavor and textureso you can eat them anyway you like. From pot bean, to salads, to soups, it's your call.

Moro

Looking a little psychedelic, or like a piece of modern artwork, the Moro bean captured my attention immediately. At first I thought they might be tepary beans, but after growing Moros I found them to be *Phaseolus vulgaris*, like most other beans in Mexico and the New World.

I've only ever seen them in Puebla (where they were erroneously labeled as Parraleño) and Hidalgo, where they're not as common but have ardent fans, including me! A friend's mother recalls eating the young plants, just after they got their first sets of leaves, sautéed with butter as a late summer treat. Dried, their colors are in full bloom and they have to be one of the prettiest, oddest beans ever.

In Mexico, I was lucky enough to be the guest of a grower, Abel. After a tour of his bean and corn fields, we went back to his house where lunch was waiting for us. I've been a guest of some of the finest chefs in the world, and I don't want to discount their great work; but this simple luncheon of Moro beans, fresh handmade tortillas, and a salad of boiled cactus paddles, tomatoes, and queso fresco, served with cold beers on a hot day, will remain one of the favorite meals of my life. They also had a searingly hot table salsa made with de Arbol chiles. Tears ran down my face and my eyes were cloudy from the spice and while I looked around in pain, and received a lot of curious sympathy for my miserable state, I don't know when I've been happier.

Phaseolus vulgaris Panamito

COLOR *and* MARKINGS Panamitos are small, round gray-cream beans with a black point in their centers.

FLAVOR *and* TEXTURE Beans like Panamitos are great for soups. As a whole bean, they can be a little like baby food, which can be unappealing. But for soups, they're incredible. You can make them as simple or elaborate as you like, vegetarian or with meat. I like to make up a soup using a simple white bean like the Panamito as a base and then empty out the fading vegetables in my refrigerator's crisper drawer to make a somewhat healthy dish. It never fails to be delicious.

Panamitos also work well as a side dish with grilled, juicy meats, where some of the meat liquid is bound to mix with the beans.

Panamito

Panamitos are small, white Alubia-style beans. They're more neutral-flavored than their Peruvian sister, Caballero, and therefore more versatile. Cultivated for hundreds of years in Peru, "frijol panamito" has been a key part of the Peruvian diet since Incan times, where they were used for stews, salads, and soups. Panamitos are such a nice, mild bean that if you're lucky enough to come across some, you can use them in almost any dish.

Peruvians have a lovely dish called frejolada, which is a rich mix of chorizo sausage, pork, and other ingredients cooked in a base of Panamito or Caballero beans.

Phaseolus vulgaris Parraleño

COLOR *and* **MARKINGS** Parraleños beans are solid brown, almost like milk chocolate.

FLAVOR *and* **TEXTURE** These beans have a very neutral taste, but they're dense and have a wonderful tooth to them. They're fine on their own or with aromatic herbs, but there's something missing that a nice piece of pork can fix. I also love the bean broth they produce, and when cooking them, I like to make sure there's enough liquid to save for later, which I use to poach eggs.

Parraleño

Puebla is an incredible city in the heart of Mexico. It's famous for its colonial buildings, Talavera ceramics, and perhaps most of all, for its food. Of course for me the highlight of a visit to Puebla is hunting for beans in the markets. The nearby market in Chalula is exceptional, even for Mexico. Inside the market buildings there are excellent bean vendors with unusual regional beans, and outside of the market, normally sitting on grass mats, are indigenous farmers selling their beans that have been passed down for generations. Normally the farmers are shy but sooner or later I get them to talk about their beans, how they grow, and how they prepare them.

On one trip I discovered Parraleños. I couldn't find them on any menu so it wasn't until I got home and cooked them did I realize how nice they are.

Phaseolus vulgaris Pusacc Punuy

COLOR *and* MARKINGS This is a multicolored bean, mostly red with pink markings. There are also some solid yellow beans and a few yellow beans with purple markings.

FLAVOR *and* TEXTURE Pusacc Punuy is incredibly rich and dense but not in a creamy or starchy way. They have a fudge-like texture and would work as a pot bean or in more elaborate recipes, but I wouldn't bother with them in salads.

Pusacc Punuy

have been lucky enough to have been served beans all my life. I've always liked them, and then of course I became a little obsessive about them. In Mexico, mothers weaning their children from breast milk will give their babies some pot liquor from the bean pot. It's easy to digest, incredibly healthy, and it starts the kids out with a love of beans.

As in a lot of families with two kids, one of my two sons isn't such an adventurous eater (to put it mildly) and the other loves oysters, gorgonzola, or just about anything else you put in front of him. I am a dedicated home cook, so my heart breaks a little each time the fussy one rejects something wonderful I've made. Believe it or not, beans haven't been as easy as they should have been for him, despite his exposure from the start. He declared he only liked pinto beans at one point so from then on, any new bean was "a new kind of pinto" and he eats heartily.

I made a bowl for The Particular Eater. I've learned to set the food down and start talking about the weather or video games—anything except the food at hand—or it becomes a showdown. He timidly started to eat and I could only look at him out of the corner of my eye, but I was relieved to see he was actually eating them, not just tasting them. I knew victory was mine when he asked, "What are these beans called?" and then my heart sank as I tried to sound as if I weren't making up the name Pusacc Punuy as I was going along!

Phaseolus vulgaris Rebosero

COLOR *and* MARKINGS Reboseros are a light purple, almost gray bean with white or gray mottling. A rebozo is a long scarf favored by Mexican women, and I wonder if the bean is the color of a local rebozo or if there was a rebozo factory nearby.

FLAVOR *and* TEXTURE Reboseros are rich and delicious and among the beans with which I insist you don't use chicken broth or too much flavoring. Onion, garlic, and maybe some olive oil, bacon fat, or lard will do.

Rebosero

After years of producing beans in California, I was really looking forward to meeting some small Mexican farmers and seeing how they raised and cleaned their crops, and, if it made sense, to eventually start importing their beans.

When my ten-year-old son Robby first tried these beautiful Rebosero beans, along with tortillas, prepared for us by the farmer in Hidalgo, it was about as delicious and pure a meal as I could hope for—except for the grilled goat, wrapped in a banana leaf, which this little American boy had never seen before. I glanced at Robby, and I could sense a little panic. Without saying a word, I urged him to keep an open mind and take one for the team, so to speak—and he did. He cautiously ate one piece of goat barbecue and then his face went red with excitement and a smile grew from ear to ear.

"It's good, Papa!" he declared, and I was both relaxed and proud.

The Roberseros were delicious, soft and almost buttery. They have a rich, soupy pot liquor that went great with the tortillas and I'd imagine they'd be fine with simple noodles. When I got home from the trip, our shipment from Maria arrived and I could taste the lunch she served us in my imagination.

Phaseolus vulgaris Rice

COLOR *and* **MARKINGS** Rice beans are white and simple and have no markings. There's something undeniably cute about them and people seem drawn to their look. Maybe it's their tiny size.

FLAVOR *and* **TEXTURE** Rice beans taste very much like a classic navy bean.

Rice

My confession is that I dislike classic navy beans. They have a baby-food texture, almost a sponginess really, and bland taste that just doesn't appeal to me. I can see how they'd be nostalgic comfort food for some, but I'll take a bowl of pintos over navys any day. Having said that, I still think there's an important place on the pantry shelf for the Rice bean, which tastes very much like a navy. This tiny little dynamo is incredibly popular with bean chefs. It cooks quickly because it's so small. It looks like a tiny grain of rice, but the flavor is that of a standard navy bean. It has more skin than a normal bean because it's so small, and this gives them a better texture than the average skins on a navy.

If the beans are from a recent harvest, they can be cooked in less than an hour. That's good news for a busy chef, but there are often better choices from a culinary point of view.

Phaseolus vulgaris Rio Zape

COLOR *and* **MARKINGS** The first thing that hits you is the lovely dark purple color of the beans. When they are cooked, the color gets darker, almost like a chocolate-purple, completely taking over the black zebra stripe markings once they're completely cooked.

FLAVOR *and* **TEXTURE** Rio Zape is very similar to a classic pinto bean, but it's more dense and exudes a deep, rich pot liquor. I don't think these work well in a lot of recipes because they are so rich and distinct. In Mexico, there's a great dish called enfrijoladas that uses pureed beans as the basis for a sauce, and like enchiladas, hot oil-doused tortillas get smothered in it. I've made this dish many times with Rio Zape and it seems born for the dish. Even still, the best way to enjoy Rio Zape is as a pot bean, perhaps with a squeeze of lime and some chopped raw white onion as a garnish. You need nothing else!

Rio Zape

When I first started growing beans, the Internet was just exploding and turning into a wonderful source of information and seeds. Seeds of Change and the Seed Savers Exchange were among my favorites, but it was Native Seeds/SEARCH that intrigued me the most. They focus on plants indigenous to Northern Mexico and the American Southwest only; and while it may seem a little shortsighted to miss out on a lot of other plants, it shows how effective narrowing your focus and concentrating on your passion can be. I take a lot of flack for not growing Old World plants. There's a lot of pressure to provide black-eyed peas for Southerners on New Year's Day, believe it or not. I like non-natives, but it's not my area of expertise and other people and companies have them well covered, it seems to me.

Rio Zape is also known as the Hopi String bean. Apparently among the Hopi, it was used as a green bean as well as a dried one. I've eaten them as green beans, but there are better heirloom varieties, like Kentucky Wonder, for that. I can still remember my first taste of Rio Zape prepared as dried beans: they were like the pintos I loved, but so much more. At first they were creamy and indulgent feeling, but there was a back flavor of chocolate and coffee, subtle but distinct.

Years later I found a bean in Mexico called San Franciscano with identical markings. The size was slightly smaller and the flavor a little more subtle, but I believe it's the same bean and another example of how great bean migration can be.

Phaseolus vulgaris Rosa de Castilla

COLOR *and* **MARKINGS** Rosa de Castilla is a pretty pink with cream-colored bubbles decorating the bean, like bubbles of champagne.

FLAVOR *and* **TEXTURE** The beans are very light and soak up whatever you cook with them. You could add pork if you like, but I still maintain a simple mirepoix is best. If you wanted to cook in the style of Michoacán (the state they hail from), you would use freshly rendered lard instead of olive oil. Once cooked, the beans stay whole and then melt in your mouth. Can you tell I'm smitten?

Rosa de Castilla

Rosa de Castilla is related to the other Central Mexican classic beans, Flor de Mayo and Flor de Junio: May Flower and June Flower, respectively. Rosa de Castilla is prettier, and I also prefer the flavor. They're much harder to find, but worth the bother. My first encounter was in a small rural market not too far from the beautiful little town of Patzcuaro. I found a very sweet older man selling this bean, and its beauty just knocked my socks off. "What do you call this one?" I asked in Spanish.

"Frijol," he replied, meaning "bean."

"Yes, I know. But what do you call it? What type?"

"It's a bean. Frijol. Frijoles." He wasn't getting mad at me, but you could see the confusion in his face." Why can't this half-wit understand?" he must have been thinking.

I looked around and saw two other vendors and they gave me the same answer. As far as they were concerned, these were what beans are, not a fancy type or a variety. In this town, beans mean Rosa de Castilla.

I couldn't wait to get home and sample them. Fortunately, they were as delicious as they were pretty and I remember thinking I was the luckiest guy on the planet because I got to go around rediscovering neglected beans. I grew them in my trial gardens in Napa with great success.

The one downside to the bean also holds true for Flor de Mayo and Flor de Junio: they don't age well. Most beans are fine if stored properly and consumed within about two years. This type of bean starts getting dense and dark and very average within one year, and it's best if you can eat them within eight months of harvest.

Phaseolus coccineus Runner Cannellini

COLOR *and* **MARKINGS** Runner Cannellinis are medium large to large oval white beans with no markings or color variations.

FLAVOR *and* **TEXTURE** Runner Cannellinis taste as if someone has added a pat of butter to each pot. They're rich and delicious, and I don't know anyone who hasn't gone nuts for them. Of course they're great as a pot bean but the Tuscan tradition of serving the cooked beans on a bed of cooked kale and tomatoes is a winner. It's chewy and creamy and it makes you wonder why we consume so much meat when things like this taste so good. Another Italian treat is to use the cooked beans in a salad with a red onion and good canned tuna.

Runner Cannellini

When I first got involved with heirlooms, it was the pinto-like varieties that captured my imagination. They were like the beans I knew, and yet so much more. Chip Morris, who had been in the bean business for years with his wife, Bobbi, kept talking about Runner Cannellini and how this was the bean the chefs clamored for, and this was the bean that was going to be a number-one seller. I tried to be polite, but I secretly thought he was a little nuts. It was a stupid white bean. Who cares when Rio Zape had hints of chocolate and the teparies tasted of the earth and you could just smell history? Well, of course, I finally cooked the large white beans and understood in an instant why these beans were so popular. Despite the fact that I had only cooked them with a little mirepoix and olive oil, they tasted like someone had buttered them and spent hours with some kind of kitchen magic. This could not be a healthy bean, with such a guilt-inducing texture and flavor.

Regular Cannellinis are basically a variant of Great Northern beans, which normally grow in a bush pattern. These are runners, meaning instead of growing in a pole or bush manner, the plant throws off long runners. They have virtually nothing to do with ordinary Cannellini beans, and from the first taste, I wished they had a different name.

You'll also hear about Gigandes from Spain and Greece, and Corona from Italy. These are all excellent beans and in fact are some variation of large white runner beans, but I love the Runner Cannellini the best. The others can have a starchy potato texture if not grown well. Runner Cannellinis can vary in size from season to season but their flavor is more consistently great.

Phaseolus vulgaris Sangre de Toro

COLOR *and* MARKINGS The fresher the beans, the redder the color; as Sangre de Toros and other red beans age, they begin to brown. Sangre de Toros tend to be round, but other red beans can be longer and thinner, like a kidney bean.

FLAVOR *and* TEXTURE Red beans tend to be dense so they don't work as well as a simple pot bean. Normally you'll find them mixed into a recipe like dirty rice or mofongo. As you might guess, their pot liquor is very good, and smart cooks love the way it coats each grain of rice.

Sangre de Toro

If you follow the health trends in the news, almost any week you are likely to read about the superior benefits of this or that bean. One report claims black beans can save your life, and then another decides it's the moment for red beans. The problem is these stories are often just sharing the obvious: beans are an incredible super food. I look often, but when one story claims red beans are the best for your health, they never seem to compare them to other beans, only other foods.

Red beans had a big moment a few years back. As you can guess, it doesn't interest me much. I love how they taste and how nice they go with sausages and other pork products for red beans and rice. In fact, you can skip the pork and still have a killer dish.

Red beans are more popular in the Caribbean and Central America than other beans, but you find some variation all over the Americas.

Phaseolus vulgaris Santa Maria Pinquito

COLOR *and* **MARKINGS** Pinquitos are a dull pink, bordering on brown. The skins look like the paper skins of Spanish peanuts. The beans are always round and consistently small from season to season.

FLAVOR *and* **TEXTURE** Santa Maria Pinks are dense and meaty, but not starchy. They make a fine pot bean, but also benefit from a good deal of fussing, as is done in a traditional Santa Maria barbecue. Additions to the beans can include mustard, molasses, chiles, and green peppers. If you're cooking them, try a small cupful plain before all the primping begins and enjoy them as a hearty pot bean.

Santa Maria Pinquito

It's thought that migrant citrus workers in Santa Maria, California, introduced Santa Maria Pinquito beans to Americans along with the cut of beef known as tri-tip. Barbecues in Santa Maria are an elaborate affair, and there are always pinquito beans involved.

Normally, it's the meat that gets the marinade and attention and the beans that are a simple unadorned side dish, but it's almost the opposite in Santa Maria. The tri-tip is flavored mostly by the act of barbecuing and it's the beans that have a miraculous transformation.

Phaseolus vulgaris Snowcap

COLOR *and* **MARKINGS** Snowcaps look like cranberry beans on steroids, dipped in white chocolate.

FLAVOR *and* **TEXTURE** Snowcaps are a prime soup bean, especially when partially pureed. They have a texture like silky potatoes and a mild flavor that would benefit from a little pork. Despite their markings, the flavor is nothing like a cranberry bean!

Snowcap

Easily one of the most dramatic looking beans, Snowcaps are the largest *Phaseolus vulgaris* variety that I've ever found. They're huge, and their lovely markings are pretty remarkable, even for a dried bean. I like to joke with our customers that my sons hand paint each and every bean. For a moment they pause, not quite sure what to say, and then laugh, nervously, when they realize I'm joking. I'd heard for years about their famous potato chowder flavor, and I wasn't disappointed when I finally had a pound to cook with.

Because of the potato similarity, I like to cook them with bacon, normally rendering some onions in the bacon fat and crumbling some bacon pieces over each bowl at the end. A few snips of chives wouldn't be inappropriate. If you've had a very bad day and need a little indulging, a pat of butter is OK by me.

I've heard many times that Snowcaps retain their markings after you cook them. I've not had such good luck. There may be some whisper of the markings left when the beans are fully cooked, but it's not going to be something to get excited about. Please make sure your beans are fully cooked!

Phaseolus vulgaris Taos Red

COLOR *and* **MARKINGS** Taos Reds are very large red beans, with dark maroon mottling and striping.

FLAVOR *and* **TEXTURE** Like most red beans, Taos Reds have a meaty interior and make good pot liquor.

Taos Red

Taos Reds are another great bean introduced to me by Native Seeds/SEARCH in Arizona. Normally, they're grown with irrigation at an elevation of 7,500 feet, but I managed to grow them fine at sea level in Napa, California. I was so excited when I first saw the plants coming up, it seems within days of planting the beans. They seemed to be going crazy and I was sure I had a super crop for my microclimate. The plants kept growing and looking healthier and healthier, and I was imagining pot after pot of New Mexican goodness. Other beans then seemed to overtake the Taos Reds and started to flower and grow bean pods while these simply had incredible foliage. Once our summer became insanely hot in Napa, as it does for a few months, the flowers arrived and these were followed by the pods. It ended up being a long growing season, but it was worth it for these great red beans.

Red beans and rice may be a natural pair, but I really love eating these beans with just some steamed cactus paddles, a dollop of salsa, and some queso fresco. I don't think you can do better than that.

Phaseolus coccineus Tarbais

COLOR *and* **MARKINGS** Tarbais is a solid cloudy white runner bean, medium to large in size. True Tarbais tend to be a little wrinkled and uneven, but this could be due more to sloppy farming than to a growing trait. It is hard to differentiate them from other white runners, such as Emergo or Runner Cannellini, except that they have more of a matte (less glossy) skin.

FLAVOR *and* **TEXTURE** The first time I ate true Tarbais, it was from the kitchen of Mediterranean food expert Paula Wolfert. My initial response was, Jacob's Cattle! They both have a slight potato texture and perhaps even a hint of the flavor. Both beans can stand the hours of cooking required for a decent cassoulet.

Tarbais

Elusive and jaw-droppingly expensive, even in their native France, Tarbais are medium-sized runner beans, similar to Runner Cannellini and from the same species as scarlet runners, making their origin in ancient Mesoamerica. In Tarbes and Camont, home of cassoulet, they are the preferred bean. In reality, there are a lot of variations in cassoulets and there are a few different beans that are used. *Larousse Gastronomique* declares Haricot Coco as the bean of choice.

As of this writing, Tarbais can cost as much as $35 a pound. While they are wonderful, you could substitute a large white runner bean in a cassoulet, and with all the sausages and duck fat, I doubt you'd really know the difference.

The French have made it illegal to use the name Tarbais for anything grown from the Tarbais bean outside of Tarbes. There's definitely a terroir issue with beans, as there is for many vegetables and clearly grapes, so it doesn't bother me much. At Rancho Gordo, we are growing ours as French Runner beans.

Phaseolus vulgaris Toloso

COLOR *and* MARKINGS The most prized (and expensive) Tolosos are shiny
black and marked by a simple white dot. There is another, unrelated bean from
the region that has a beautiful rust-red background and yellow flecks that is sus-
piciously close to the Colombian Cargamanto bean. Personally I prefer the red,
but I'd be happy with a trip to Spain and a big sack of each in my luggage.

FLAVOR *and* TEXTURE These beans are very hearty, and traditionalists do
not soak them. Extremists are said to only cook them in fresh rainwater and rush
outside with various pots when it starts to pour. They can stand up to additions
of pork, chorizo, and spices.

Toloso, Red and Black

When someone says "Spain," you may think of castles, paella, or Don Quixote. I think of Toloso beans.

Toloso beans originated in the Basque province of Gipúzkoa, Spain, a mountain town just outside of San Sebastian. This highly prized bean has been grown since ancient times. Along with the Toloso bean, the area is also known for manufacturing the popular Basque berets.

The bean often grows alongside crops like guindilla, a small green pepper, corn, and apples for cider—essentially the three sisters method.

Phaseolus vulgaris Vallarta

COLOR *and* **MARKINGS** Vallartas are solid yellow with a slight green cast when super fresh.

FLAVOR *and* **TEXTURE** Vallartas are rich and thick. I wouldn't want a big bowl of them as a meal, but cut with bitter greens, they're great. I once pureed a batch and used it as filling in ravioli, along with a sage leaf and a small amount of butter. That was a huge hit!

Vallarta

was told the original Vallarta came from the state of Jalisco. I liked it but mostly because when really fresh, it has a slight green shade to it. When I first cooked it, I was underwhelmed and in fact didn't really like the super-thick, almost peanut butter texture of the bean. I later tried it with mixed bitter greens and fell in love with it. Is it possible a vegetable can be too rich?

This bean was mentioned earlier as being one of the favorites of Chef Thomas Keller from the French Laundry here in the Napa Valley and Per Se restaurant in Manhattan. There's nothing that makes me happier than the thought of some obscure, near extinct bean, considered a lowly Depression-era food of the poor, being served with pride at two of the world's finest restaurants.

Phaseolus vulgaris Vaqueros

COLOR *and* MARKINGS There are dozens of "cow" beans, but I think Vaquero wins for having the most realistic markings. The spots are black and white, with a slight lead going to the blacks.

FLAVOR *and* TEXTURE A good chili bean needs to be able to stand up to the fire of the chili sauce and the chewiness of the beef. Ideally, the bean would have heartier pot liquor that would add to the chili sauce, and Vaqueros win in all counts.

Vaqueros

When it comes to beans and chili, the following question is a dealmaker: do you add beans to a classic chili con carne? In Texas, where a "bowl of red" is serious business, the answer is no. But to serve chili without beans on the side would be even weirder than including beans in the dish. Personally, I like my chili thin and soupy, with no tomatoes, lots of beef and some beans. I don't normally care for the stodgy mess you find in a can that seems to be more about beans and ground beef than chili. Oh well, to each his own.

Vaqueros are a classic chili bean. I've been told that they are a cross between Anasazi beans and pintos, but I'm not so sure. I do love their texture in a bowl of chili, and I also love them on their own. When they are super fresh, within a few months of harvest, the pot liquor is thin and inky black, which is fun.

Phaseolus vulgaris Vermont Cranberry

COLOR *and* **MARKINGS** Vermont Cranberry has the same odd, mottled markings as any cranberry bean, but it also looks as if someone has dipped it for some reason into a vat of lilac dye.

FLAVOR *and* **TEXTURE** I don't know if I could tell any of the cranberry beans apart blindfolded, but I do love their silky texture.

Vermont Cranberry

Growing up on the West Coast, I never really caught what I call "Baked Bean Fever." Baked beans make a nice dish, but on the East Coast, aficionados are like martini drinkers in their exacting standards and techniques. An old time New Englander would like nothing more than to tell you his exact recipe for making baked beans and show you the clay crock to cook them in. Again, I'm a Native Son of the Golden West, so I won't be offended if you want to correct me, but nine times out of ten, recipes for baked beans call for Jacob's Cattle. The Vermont Cranberry is an old-time American heirloom dating back to the 1700s that our Vermont brothers and sisters insist is the only bean for baked beans. Besides their delicious flavor and their attractive velvety texture, cranberry beans can handle long, slow cooking without falling apart.

Phaseolus vulgaris Yellow Eye

COLOR *and* **MARKINGS** Yellow Eyes are a pure white bean with a yellow splotch around the eye—the fresher the bean, the more intense the yellow, which can turn almost brown on older beans.

FLAVOR *and* **TEXTURE** Yellow Eyes have a potato-like texture, but their flavor is more chowdery. They hold their own against strong pork products and are really one of the best heirloom varieties.

Yellow Eye

Traditionally, Yellow Eyes have been the bean of choice for regional baked bean aficionados. Their russet potato texture is a perfect mix with classic baked bean ingredients, and distinctly different from the other regional preference, Vermont Cranberry. I've also heard of Yellow Eyes subbing for black-eyed peas in the classic Southern dish Hoppin' John, eaten on New Year's Day to insure luck for the rest of the year. The first time I tasted Yellow Eyes, I immediately thought this would be a ham hock's best friend. In fact, I normally cook my beans vegetarian, but this is the bean I reach for when I have a good bit of pork. Yet a French friend has declared these are his favorite beans of all, and a simple mirepoix and olive oil were all he added when preparing them. I think in the end, this is simply a great bean and very easy to like. We grow and sell tons of them each year.

Phaseolus vulgaris Yellow Indian Woman

COLOR *and* **MARKINGS** Yellow Indian Woman beans are small, milky yellow, and round. They have no markings.

FLAVOR *and* **TEXTURE** The flavor of Yellow Indian Woman is fairly mild. The real interest is in the texture. I have a theory that people love beans like this because they give you the same feeling you get when you're eating a creamy, high-fat food. You can puree them, maybe add a little anchovy or a small bit of butter and the result is similar to eating a good triple-cream cheese, without the same fat or calorie content.

Yellow Indian Woman

At the farmers markets, Yellow Indian Woman gets an incredible amount of attention, which is nice but odd considering it's solid yellow, small, and has no interesting markings. Maybe it's the name or the pretty yellow color. Whatever it is, cooks are always a little surprised when they finally bite into the beans. I remember laughing at how creamy they were. I was expecting something a little starchier and boring, not this luxurious release of bean heaven. They remind me a lot of black turtle beans and would make a great substitute, especially in dishes like black bean chili.

One restaurant I know refuses to call them by their name. One would assume the beans were grown by an Indian woman at one point, hence their name— but I don't think it was meant to be racist! Their origins can be traced to Montana, and their less-common name is Buckeye beans.

Because of the short Montana growing season, Yellow Indian Woman has been bred to grow fast and plentiful. You can almost watch the vines grow by standing in the bean fields on a summer day. Well, maybe not quite, but they are fast and prolific, sometimes allowing us to get two harvests in a single, long summer.

TIP Try making these beans with a base of freshly rendered lard, white onions, garlic, and nothing else. The beans really soak up the flavors beautifully.

Phaseolus vulgaris Zebra

COLOR *and* MARKINGS Zebra beans have a tan base and black, zebra-like markings.

FLAVOR *and* TEXTURE Zebras seem to be a cross between a classic pinto and a brown bean. They have a slight nutty flavor as well.

Zebra

Zebra beans are one of those varieties that make a great green bean along with being a terrific dry bean. You can plant them for just pods and seed saving, and you'll be rewarded with pretty green pods with blue streaks on them. Take it a little further and let them get to the drying stage and the pods go from green and blue to white, and beans inside the now-brittle pod morph from white to creamy tan beans with distinct zebra-like markings. It's the kind of vegetable that you'll find rewarding for the flavor and the kids will get an endless kick out of just for the looks. Between the way it looks and the name, you can't lose. It's little tricks like these that get kids interested in gardening and food.

As a dry bean, they're fairly creamy. I've read that they're popular in Spain but I've never been able to confirm this. I eat them, like most good heirlooms, fairly plain. A drizzle of sunflower oil at the end is nice.

The Zebra bean is also known as the amethyst bean.

Phaseolus vulgaris Zolfino

COLOR *and* **MARKINGS** Zolfini beans are small, round, and yellow, with soft skins.

FLAVOR *and* **TEXTURE** In Italy, they are eaten boiled (pot style), dressed with extra virgin olive oil, and piled on toasted bread or served as a side dish

Zolfino

If Tarbais are the most mystical of beans in France, the Italian version has to be the Zolfino bean (Zolfini, plural). Ask Tuscans about this bean, and their eyes water slightly and their mouths go dry at the memory of their favorite legume. It's very funny.

The beans are indeed delicious, but I'll admit that the first time I ate them I was a little disappointed. They are incredibly mild, almost to the point of being bland. But the point is the way they melt and the way they showcase the excellent Tuscan olive oil. Classic "beans on toast" reaches a new level when you make it with properly cooked Zolfini beans and top-of-the-line olive oil. It's great hangover food, too.

My friend Judy Wits-Francini, who runs a cooking school and offers gastronomic tours in Tuscany, always comes home to San Francisco with bags of Zolfini for me. Apparently there are some farmers who are using poor seed and the wrong technique to grow a second-rate version of the Zolfino and Judy is working with legacy farmers to make sure people get to experience the true bean instead of a pale imitation. On her last visit, she made them with just sage, roasted tomatoes, and some simple Italian sausage. It sounds so basic, but I found myself eating bowl after bowl of this seemingly magical potion.

Cooking Beans, Rancho Gordo Style

The idea of cooking dried beans can be a little intimidating. How is it possible that these seemingly bone-dry "rocks," no matter how pretty, will actually turn into the creamy, indulgent beans we crave? Too many home cooks have had bad experiences with beans either turning to mush, or perhaps more commonly, refusing to cook through. A new cook isn't likely to want to take on a job that can take hours when there is a chance they will be looking at an inedible pot of nastiness.

First off, I have to tell you that yes, beans can take a long time to cook. In fact, the lower the heat and the slower the cooking, the more likely you'll have a memorable bean. While cooking beans can take hours, it's not like cooking risotto, where you have to tend to the dish nearly every minute by constant stirring. In fact, you can elect to cook the beans in an electric slow cooker and leave the house altogether. Slow-cooking beans can be pleasant and leisurely if you make a habit of it; it's a time you'll be looking forward to all week.

Next, you'll want to pay close attention to the quality of your beans. Knowing your producer and when the beans have been harvested will help you find the best quality of beans. Look for beans that have been harvested within two years, within one year being even better. Beyond two years, and the flavor starts to deteriorate and the beans take seemingly forever to cook; or worse, they never soften.

If you live in an urban area with lots of Latinos or East Indians buying pulses, it's much easier to get a good product. If you're in the Midwest and buying Baby Limas in a plastic sack at a typical grocery store, it's less likely that these beans are under two years old. The best-case scenario is to find a local source, which isn't always practical. There are several bean sources available online (see Resources at the back of this book), including a popular website called Rancho Gordo. I hear the owner is particularly good-looking! Latino food stores or stores that specialize in products from India are also likely to have fresher stock. They often don't have the most interesting selection, but it's always worth checking out.

In the kitchen at Rancho Gordo.

After you've purchased your beans, hopefully fresh and of an heirloom variety, you want to check them for small stones, pebbles, and organic debris. Most of the bean cleaning happens right in the field, but even with modern "triple-cleaned" technology, there's a chance there's some dirt among your beans. So hunt for junk and then rinse well in several changes of water.

After they are cleaned, I like to soak the beans. Most cooks in Mexico don't soak their beans; most cooks in Europe do. Soaking speeds up the cooking time, but of course it delays it as well (since the time you save on cooking, you spend on soaking!). Soaking overnight is a common solution, but that means you're going to need to start cooking first thing in the morning. You can soak for 24 hours but I've had fresh beans (dried beans within a year old) actually start to harden from too much soaking. My recommendation is to soak your beans from two to six hours when possible; and if you can't, just start cooking. Some folks like to change the soaking water; I don't. For every food scientist who believes changing the water will help your digestion, there's another who thinks the effect of changing the water is so minimal that it's not worth it, and that potentially you are throwing healthy aspects of the beans down the drain. You will find that old-time bean cookers are rather adamant in their instructions and allow little room for discussion. This is fine. If you want to soak for eight hours and then change the water, it's not the end of the world. The main thing is that you're cooking beans!

Now it's time to choose your pot. An enameled cast-iron pot, like the Le Creuset line from France, is ideal; a good stockpot works fine as well. Heat about 3 tablespoons of olive oil in the pot and sauté some finely chopped onion, garlic, celery, and carrots. If you're missing one of these aromatic vegetables, don't worry. Make do with what you have on hand. I've seen chefs cut up the vegetables (or mirepoix) into chunks, but I like mine rather fine and I like them to almost dissolve into the beans. Once the vegetables are soft, add the cleaned beans and enough water to cover them by one inch if they were soaked, and two inches if they are straight from the bag. You can cook them in the soaking water or not, whatever your instincts tell you.

Beans cook better and faster if you leave half of the pot empty. In other words, don't fill the pot all the way up to the top with beans; save almost half the pot for room to circulate moist air.

Speaking of instincts, you may feel compelled to add chicken stock instead of plain water. I understand this temptation but I suggest you resist if you are cooking fresh, dried, heirloom beans from a good grower.

I love meat and don't see myself being a vegetarian any time soon (never say never!) but the fact is, you've paid a premium price for these lovely legumes and I want you to experience them on their own as an ingredient. Beans are mild, but they are delicious and while the aromatic vegetables we've used complement the natural flavor of beans, the chicken stock is going to overwhelm them. It will be good, but if you're using good beans, I challenge you to tell me if it's better. It simply isn't! The same goes for a ham hock. I love the pork and beans combination and if I had a ham hock, I'd probably reach for Yellow Eye beans. But the first time you cook them, I beg you to try them more au natural.

After you've added the beans and water to the pot, turn up the heat to medium high and bring the liquid to a rapid boil. Once it is boiling, let it continue for five to fifteen minutes. Turn the heat down to low. After the rapid boiling, we just want the beans to gently simmer until they've finished cooking. I prefer to use a heat diffuser and bring the fire down to as low as it will go and let the beans cook undisturbed for hours. The lid of the pot should come off and on as needed to control the simmering. If you're in a hurry, make the simmer a bit more lively, but be aware that the beans might be a little uneven and you may have more bean breakdown than you want.

Now you can pretty much leave the beans alone and watch a good movie on TV or work on the rest of the dinner if you're ambitious. At one point, the pot will smell less and less like the aromatic vegetables and more and more like beans. If you test one, you'll see that it's softening, even if it still has a ways to go. This is when I salt my beans. It's almost as if there's been a battle between the beans and me and this is the moment of no return for the beans. I have won. I will now salt them.

You want to salt as soon as you can so that there's time for the salt to penetrate the bean's interior. Otherwise you'll just have salty water and under-seasoned beans. Traditional folklore tells us that salt actually toughens beans. I haven't found this to be true. I've experimented and added the salt up front and there's been no negative effect, but I still don't trust salting too early. I'm too cheap to waste a pot of beans and after all these years of cooking beans, I just can't salt them right off the bat.

While the beans are cooking, keep an eye on them. You may need to add more water. Another bit of kitchen folklore is that you need to add hot water or the beans will harden, but I add room-temperature water all the time and have never noticed the beans taking longer to cook. Once the beans are finished, you should be able to blow on the surface of a bean and the skin will wrinkle. Or you could just pop one in your mouth. Beans should have some texture, but they should never be crunchy or too al dente.

If you want to add tomatoes, limes, vinegar, molasses, or some other acidic ingredient, you should wait until the beans are thoroughly cooked. Acid toughens the skin, not to the point where the beans will never soften, but it delays the process a lot and actually changes the texture of the beans.

HOW TO COOK BEANS

So there! You've made beans. I've given you a lot of little nuanced tips, but let's review the basics:

1. Check the beans for debris and rinse in several changes of water.

2. Sauté aromatic vegetables in olive oil.

3. Add the beans and enough liquid to cover by one inch if soaked, two inches if not soaked.

4. Bring the pot to a rapid boil for 5 to 15 minutes.

5. Lower the heat to a gentle simmer until the beans are done, between an hour and three hours.

6. Salt when the beans are just starting to turn soft.

COOKING IN CLAY

I had seen clay pots in Mexico and Italy, but it never dawned on me that I'd want one until I met Paula Wolfert. She's known the world over for her seminal books on Mediterranean cuisines and if you ever encounter her, you will get caught up in her enthusiasm. One of her passions is clay pots, and several years ago, she got me so hooked that now I can't imagine a trip home from Europe or Mexico without something clay and fragile on my lap during the plane ride.

Mexicans cook with clay all the time and their low-fired pots go right on the gas stove or over charcoals. Each clay piece is different and imparts a particular flavor, even when glazed. When cooking in clay, you are forced to cook slowly and at low temperatures; no ingredient benefits more from this than beans.

All of the techniques mentioned earlier can be applied to clay pot cooking, except for the high heat. Clay is a great conductor of heat and you'll find you don't really need the extreme temperatures. The key is to make changes in the fire slowly, so that you don't shock the pot.

I even sauté the aromatics in oil directly in my clay pots. Within seconds, the oil starts bubbling, cooking the mirepoix as if in a frying pan.

Knock on wood— I've only broken one of my clay pieces; and that was by dropping it, not from cooking in it!

Mexican clay pots.
STEVE SANDO

SLOW COOKER

Another, perhaps more practical, manner of cooking beans is in the slow cooker. You'll need to sauté the vegetables in a pan and add them to the cooker, along with your beans and the water. I've found that most slow cookers are different, even among the same brands. The first time you cook with yours, you'll want to be home to observe how it performs. Some run very hot and some seem a little slower. In general, with freshly harvested heirloom beans, you can put them into the pot in the morning on high and arrive home from work to a glorious pot of beans, with no soaking. Most of the newer models start at high for a certain number of hours and then switch to warm. You'll need to play with yours a bit to find the sweet spot.

The one disadvantage of the slow cooker is the lack of evaporation. They need their lids on to perform the way they were intended to, so once you get home, immediately remove the lid, give the beans a stir and allow them to breathe and reduce for another hour if you can. This would be the right time to salt the beans as well, if you haven't already.

PRESSURE COOKER

Yet another technique for cooking beans is in the pressure cooker. I've previously stated that I don't recommend them and I have many good people who would like to bonk me over the head with their pressure cookers for taking this stance.

First, the good news: without soaking, you can have cooked beans within an hour of deciding to make them. That's pretty amazing. Take your cleaned beans and add some aromatic

Mushroom and bean tacos.

vegetables and some oil. (The oil is added both for flavor and also to prevent your safety valve from getting stopped up, which apparently can happen with some models.) Cook the beans at high pressure for twenty minutes, then slowly release the top and cook for another twenty minutes with the lid off, which will breathe some life back into the beans and reduce the pot liquor, making for a better pot of beans.

While this method works fine, the bean texture tends to be denser than it is when cooking them as pot beans. This isn't always a bad thing, and in fact, when you're making a pureed soup or refried beans, it doesn't matter at all.

I'm a huge fan of Lorna Sass and her seminal books on pressure cooking and whole grains. She gave me a wonderful modern pressure cooker and I had a great time cooking chuck roasts and risotto. On a whim, I tried beans again. I cooked them for twenty minutes and then slow-released them. To my surprise, the beans were soft and lovely, not as dense and thick as I'd expected. The problem was the bean broth, which had not reduced well. I added salt and returned the beans to heat, without a lid or pressure, to allow the salt to enter the beans and the broth to evaporate some. Eventually this did the trick, but it dawned on me that by the time the pot liquor had reduced enough to take on some flavor, almost another hour had gone by and I might as well have cooked them like I usually do.

While I'm open to possibilities of the pressure cooker, I'm still not convinced. The final chapter has yet to been written on this subject.

Recipes

CHAPTER

A cupboard in the Rancho Gordo kitchen.

White Bean Puree

2 cups Runner Cannellini beans, cooked and drained

¼ cup extra virgin olive oil

4 garlic cloves, roasted

1 cup parsley, chopped

2–3 tablespoons rosemary, chopped

Salt and freshly ground pepper to taste

1 tablespoon fresh lemon juice

SERVES 18-20

As you might imagine, when I'm invited to a party and asked to bring a dish, I bring beans. What else? I love preparing them in my vegetarian manner with just some olive oil and aromatic vegetables and have everyone swoon, from meat eaters to vegans alike. Despite having hundreds of recipes at my disposal, I still prefer to make and serve a pure pot of beans, as a side dish or main course. Clearly, I am a fool for beans.

One too many car ride, with my pots of beans tipping over while making a sharp turn or sudden stop, made my rethink my potluck participation. I once went to a picnic and spilled half of the beans all over the upholstery in my car. It was a hot day in a rural setting and let's just say I still have an aromatic memory of the event despite numerous car washings and air fresheners. That foul smell taught me a lesson! Now I bring dips, which aren't nearly such precarious passengers; and they're a novel way to enjoy some healthy beans.

Note: You may substitute any creamy, meaty bean, such as Marrow, Cellini, or Flageolet, for the Runner Cannellinis.

Cook the beans according to the instructions on page 150, then drain and reserve the broth. Place the drained beans in a large bowl and gently mash with a potato masher. Place the beans in a bowl of a food processor or blender and puree, adding a little of the reserved broth as needed until slightly smooth.

Add olive oil and puree until very smooth. Add the roasted garlic, parsley, rosemary, and salt and pepper to taste. Check seasoning and add lemon juice to taste. Serve on assorted crackers or crostini.

Drunken Beans, or Borrachos

4 cups pinto beans,
cooked, in their broth

1 bottle lager beer

2 slices high-quality lean bacon,
diced

½ medium yellow onion, chopped

3 garlic cloves, finely chopped

3–4 serrano chiles,
seeded if desired and chopped

1 cup button mushrooms, chopped

Salt and freshly ground
black pepper to taste

Corn tortillas, warmed for serving

Lime wedges, for serving

SERVES 4

Like many slow-cooked dishes, drunken beans taste best the next day. The bacon and beer have a better chance to seep into the beans themselves, instead of just flavoring the bean broth.

More and more, real cotija cheese from Mexico is becoming available in stores. I haven't found a decent domestic version, but I can assure you the imported cheese is sublime. Some recipes will have you substitute feta if you can't find cotija, but that's because the recipe author has never had the real thing. Real cotija is closer to Parmesan than feta. If you find it, dust each bowl with a generous amount of cotija right before serving.

Note: You may substitute Rio Zape, Red Appaloosa, or Anasazi beans for the pintos.

Cook the beans according to the instructions on page 150, reserving the broth. In a stockpot over medium heat, warm the beans and their broth. Add the beer and simmer to cook off some of the beer, about 20 minutes.

Meanwhile, in a small, heavy skillet over medium heat, sauté the bacon until the fat is nearly rendered and the bacon is brown, about 10 minutes. Remove the bacon with a slotted spoon and drain on paper towels. Pour off all but 1 tablespoon of the fat in the pot. Add the onion, garlic, and chiles and sauté over medium high heat until soft and fragrant, about 10 minutes. Add the mushrooms and sauté until wilted and soft, about 5 minutes. Stir in the cooked bacon.

Add the mushroom mixture to the beans, season with salt and pepper and simmer until the flavors are blended, about 10 minutes.

Serve the beans with warm tortillas and lime wedges.

ARAM CHAKERIAN

"We're bringing back something that has been lost."

One of our favorite customers at the Rancho Gordo shop in Napa—and before that, a longtime regular at our farmers market stands—is the multi-talented Aram Chakerian, a trained chef and licensed contractor who's worked in both the restaurant and property-development fields. In 2008, Chakerian found the perfect job for his unusual combination of skills and experience when he became the manager of the Oxbow Public Market, a spacious, modern complex on the bank of the "oxbow" curve in the Napa River that has given its name to the whole neighborhood. "I'm managing a building that's all about food," says Chakerian. Inspired by the successful redevelopment of the San Francisco Ferry Building, the Oxbow market brings small food producers and purveyors face-to-face with their customers—not only Napa visitors, who come from around the world, but local chefs and regular folks who have made it a regular stop on their food-shopping, dining-out, and socializing rounds. I'm one of them: Not a week goes by that I'm not buying sausage or duck confit at the Fatted Calf charcuterie, or spice blends like harissa from Whole Spice—two of the family-owned small businesses in the Oxbow market. More likely than not, I'll spot Chakerian on his rounds. His pedometer logs more than five miles a day as he walks through the market buildings, making sure the tenants have what they need and that all the Oxbow facilities—from the restrooms to the lighting and landscaping—are operating smoothly. Chakerian also walks to work from his home, just one block west of Rancho Gordo, and he's been a regular at the shop ever since we opened our doors. Originally from New Mexico, he grew up eating beans: pinto beans, pinto beans, and more pinto beans. "That was all we had," he says.

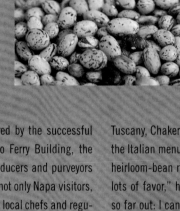

"Even lentils were exotic. I didn't have lentils until I got to France." That was in his senior year as a political-science major at the University of New Mexico, when he decided he preferred cooking to policy and, after graduating, moved to San Francisco to attend the California Culinary Academy.

In California, Chakerian's cooking horizon expanded still further when he discovered black beans: "They were a revelation to me, and those were just run-of-the-mill beans," he recalls. Then he sampled his first heirlooms, and he's never looked back. As a chef in Bay Area restaurants, including three of the popular Piatti eateries and Napa's Tuscany, Chakerian started out with Borlottis—perfect for the Italian menus he was creating. He's been widening his heirloom-bean repertoire ever since. "Obviously they have lots of favor," he says, "but also, you don't have to plan so far out: I can actually get them, bring them home, and have them for lunch the same day, which is amazing." Chakerian regularly cooks up lunchtime meals of beans in his office slow-cooker, starting them when he arrives in the morning and simmering them slowly with Mexican oregano, a touch of garlic, and some cumin. "I just bring a Zip-loc bag of dried beans with me, with all the ingredients in the bag," he explains. "Then all I have to do is add salt and pepper after they're done." With Fatted Calf just across a small parking lot from his Oxbow office, Chakerian adds, he can easily add their fabulous duck confit to some slow-cooked Flageolets for an on-the-job cassoulet. Like me, Chakerian puts flavor first. But he also finds a vital kinship between preserving heirloom beans and sustaining the family-farm philosophy that the Oxbow Public Market seeks to represent. "We're bringing back something that has been lost," he says.

Traditional Baked Beans

1 pound Vermont Cranberry beans, soaked and drained, liquid reserved

¼ pound high-quality, lean applewood smoked bacon, cut into 2-inch pieces

1 yellow onion, chopped

3 tablespoons brown sugar

1 teaspoon dry mustard

1 teaspoon salt

½ teaspoon fresh ground black pepper

½ cup molasses

SERVES 6

Growing up in California, I never quite understood baked beans. How could they compete with my favorite refried pintos? Why would someone take forever and a day to prepare beans that seemed so thick and stodgy? Well, I was eating canned baked beans in California, what did I expect? Eating the real thing, like the variation presented here, will quickly change anyone's mind.

Preheat oven to 300 degrees F.

In a 2-quart bean pot or ceramic casserole, sauté the bacon pieces over medium heat until fat begins to render. Remove all but 2 tablespoons of the bacon fat. Add the onion and sauté until softened but not browned, 6–8 minutes.

Add the brown sugar, mustard, black pepper, and molasses to the onion and bacon mixture and cook until well combined.

Add drained beans and stir until well combined. Add enough of the soaking liquid to cover the beans.

Bake covered in oven for 1½ to 2 hours. Check periodically to make sure that the beans are covered with liquid, adding more as necessary. Do not stir, to avoid breaking the beans apart.

Red Beans and Rice

2 tablespoons lard

1 yellow onion, chopped

2 garlic cloves, finely chopped

½ bunch scallions, chopped

1 pound red beans,
such as Sangre de Toros, soaked,
liquid reserved

1 pound good smoked sausage,
cut into 2-inch pieces

Salt and freshly ground
black pepper to taste

½ bunch parsley, chopped

2–4 cups cooked white rice

Sausages and beans are a marriage made in heaven. Any kind of pork in general works, but sausages are just about perfection. The great thing about this simple recipe is that you can change the beans and change the sausages and get a completely different flavor. Hopefully you have some artisan sausages at your disposal.

Sauté onions, scallions, and garlic in lard until softened. Add the beans and soaking liquid and simmer for an hour or so. Check occasionally to make sure there is enough liquid and add more as necessary.

Add salt and continue cooking until beans are soft. Remove one cup of beans; drain and mash them in a bowl. Return to the pot and combine beans thoroughly. Add the sausage and continue simmering until the sausage is heated through. Check for seasoning. Add parsley and serve over white rice.

SERVES 4-6

Good Mother Stallard Chili, à la Cindy Lou

1 pound Good Mother Stallard
beans, soaked and cooked

2 tablespoons olive oil

1½ pounds lean ground beef

1 large yellow onion,
finely chopped

2 cloves garlic, finely diced

2 cans diced tomatoes with juice

½ cup water

¼ cup apple cider vinegar

2 tablespoons balsamic vinegar

1 tablespoon salt

4 tablespoons cumin

4 tablespoons
dried Mexican oregano

4 tablespoons chile powder

1 tablespoon paprika

4 tablespoons brown sugar

SERVES 4-6

Susan Sanchez is our general manager at Rancho Gordo, as well as an excellent cook who first found success in the food world at Joyce Goldstein's seminal Square One restaurant in San Francisco (where she also found her husband, Miguel!)

A woman who worked in the building next door once came in to Rancho Gordo for some mundane thing and looked Susan in the eye and said, "Cindy? It's Cindy, right?" and now poor Susan has the nickname of Cindy, which has morphed into Cindy Lou; and at once, you understand the corporate culture at Rancho Gordo.

This is Cindy Lou's excellent chili.

Cook the beans according to the instructions on page 150. In a large heavy skillet, sauté ground beef in olive oil until browned, about 5–7 minutes. Add the onion and garlic and continue cooking until soft.

Add this mixture to the pot of beans; then add the tomatoes, ½ cup water, and vinegars. Add the salt, remaining spices, and brown sugar and mix until thoroughly combined. Simmer on low for several hours, checking occasionally to make sure liquid content is adequate. Add more water if necessary.

*Freshly ground
chile powder.*
STEVE SANDO

Mayacoba Bean Salad with Roasted Cherry Tomatoes, Lemon, and Basil

3 cups cooked and drained
Mayacoba beans (1 cup dry)

2 cups cherry tomatoes

6 tablespoons extra virgin olive oil

Salt

Pepper

1 medium shallot, finely minced

2 tablespoons red wine vinegar

1 tablespoon lemon juice

Zest of 1 large lemon

6 large basil leaves, slivered

SERVES 6

Sara Scott worked for many years at the Robert Mondavi Winery, and very quietly she's been behind the scenes defining "wine country cuisine" in the Napa Valley. She will groan when she reads this, but I don't care. She's incredibly talented, has a killer laugh, and she's a lover of good beans. What's not to like? This is her bean salad, and I consider it a favorite.

Preheat oven to 350 degrees F and position a rack in the center of the oven.

Cook beans according to the instructions on page 150; drain and set aside.

Cut the cherry tomatoes in half diagonally and place in a bowl. Toss the tomatoes with 2 tablespoons olive oil, ½ teaspoon salt and ¼ teaspoon pepper. Spread the tomatoes out in a single layer on a baking sheet and roast for 30–35 minutes, or until they start to shrivel and caramelize. Cool to room temperature.

Place the shallots, red wine vinegar, lemon juice and ½ teaspoon of salt in a small nonreactive bowl. Stir to combine. Let the mixture sit for at least 15 minutes. Stir in the lemon zest, ¼ teaspoon pepper, and the remaining 4 tablespoons olive oil.

Place the cooked beans in a medium-sized bowl. Add the roasted cherry tomatoes and the shallot mixture and gently stir to combine. Stir in the slivered basil. Taste for seasoning, adding more lemon juice or salt if needed.

Pinto Bean Pie

1 cup cranberry beans,
cooked and mashed

⅓ cup butter, softened

2 eggs, lightly beaten

¾ cup sugar

½ cup flaked coconut

1 unbaked 9-inch pie pastry shell

Whipped topping, if desired

SERVES 6

Asian cuisines have a lot of sweet adzuki bean recipes but here in the West, beans tend to be savory. In general, I prefer savory beans, but I still have dreams of the pinto bean pies we used to get from the now-defunct Your Black Muslim Bakery in Oakland. These pies were sublime, and I wish I had the exact recipe. This one is very good; there's something wonderfully weird and different about the beans' texture combined with sugar. Another similar, old-time favorite from Texas is honey beans: freshly cooked pintos are drizzled with honey for a tasty snack.

Preheat oven to 350 degrees F.

Cook the beans according to instructions on page 150; drain and mash with a bean or potato masher. Set aside. In a large bowl, combine the eggs, sugar, and butter until light and fluffy. Add the mashed beans and mix well. Gradually add the coconut. Pour this mixture into the unbaked pie shell.

Bake for 40 to 45 minutes, or until a toothpick inserted in the center comes out clean.

Let pie cool, and serve with whipped topping if desired.

LEFT *Eighteen hens and one very happy rooster.*
BELOW *Eggs from the hen house.*

Refried Beans

2 cups pinto beans, cooked,
broth reserved

3 tablespoons lard (or bacon fat)

½ white onion, sliced thin

Salt

SERVES 4

Simple, pureed beans are very good—the texture is smooth and silky and the flavor changes as the skins incorporate into the mix. Even better are proper refried beans.

Cook the beans according to the directions on page 150, reserving the broth. In a large, heavy skillet sauté the onions in the lard, with a little salt, until well-cooked and translucent, but not browned.

Add the beans and their liquid. Take a wooden bean masher or a metal potato masher and, starting at one end of the skillet, rub the beans across the bottom of the pan to the other side. The mashed beans will incorporate the liquid and the onions. Leaving a few of the beans whole for texture is very nice. Take your time, and keep mashing until you reach your desired consistency.

Black Bean Soup with Chorizo

1 medium yellow onion, chopped

1 jalapeño pepper, charred, peeled, seeds and veins removed, finely chopped

3 cloves garlic, minced

1 pound black beans, soaked, liquid reserved

1 tablespoon lard or extra virgin olive oil

1 teaspoon cumin

1 teaspoon chile powder

1 teaspoon dried Mexican oregano

Salt and freshly ground black pepper to taste

1 pound smoked chorizo, chopped

2 tablespoon cilantro, finely chopped

Lime wedges

Fresh corn tortillas

SERVES 4-6

While I was growing up, pot beans meant pintos; salad beans were red kidneys from a can, maybe some garbanzos as well if it were a big party and the opening of a second can was justi-fied. I remember distinctly being served a bowl of black bean soup in a restaurant in Santa Rosa and just falling in love. Black beans had that something extra that was undeniable. After a time, they became very popular and now they're as common as pintos.

Black beans have a creaminess and tooth like no other bean. They're versatile and delicious. There isn't a good substitute, but finding them shouldn't be much trouble.

Sauté onion and jalapeño (check for heat and if extra hot, use only part of the pepper) in lard. When onion has softened, add the garlic and cook until fragrant.

Add beans and reserved liquid and bring to a hard boil for 5 minutes. Continue cooking until beans are almost tender, about 40 minutes to an hour. Add cumin, chile powder, oregano, and salt and pepper to taste. Continue cooking until beans are cooked through, adding more water as needed for broth.

Sauté chorizo in 1 tablespoon of lard until nicely browned then add to the beans mixture and taste for seasoning. Add cilantro; then serve in bowls with lime wedges and fresh corn tortillas.

Kale and White Bean Soup

1 medium onion,
coarsely chopped

2 carrots, finely chopped

2 stalks celery, finely, chopped

1 fennel bulb, finely chopped

2 tablespoons extra virgin
olive oil, plus more for drizzling

2 cloves garlic, minced

1 pound white beans, soaked,
liquid reserved

Parmigiano-Reggiano, shredded
plus small piece cheese rind

1–2 teaspoons salt

Pinch cayenne

Freshly ground black pepper

1 pound smoked sausage,
such as kielbasa,
cut crosswise into ½ inch pieces

1 pound kale, leaves removed
from stems, coarsely chopped

Zest of ½ lemon

1 tablespoon fresh thyme,
finely chopped

SERVES 4-6

Once you start digging through hundreds of bean recipes, white beans and kale becomes almost cliché; but its popularity is for good reason. The chewiness and slight bitterness of the kale makes the fat, plump white beans seem all the more indulgent.

This is an easy dish to improvise with. Try different greens, and omit the sausage if you prefer. If you don't include meat, try toasted walnuts or pine nuts as a garnish.

Sauté onion, carrot, celery, and fennel in 3 tablespoons olive oil, over medium heat, until softened but not brown. Add garlic and cook until fragrant.

Add beans and reserved soaking liquid. Bring to boil for 5 minutes, then reduce heat to a simmer, add Parmigiano-Reggiano rind, and cook until beans are softened. When beans are almost fully cooked, add 1 teaspoon salt, cayenne, and freshly ground pepper to taste. Remove cheese rind.

While beans are cooking, sauté kielbasa in olive oil until caramelized. Set aside.

Add kale to bean mixture, adding more water if needed, and continue cooking until kale is tender. Add lemon zest, thyme, and kielbasa.

Check for seasoning and serve with a drizzle of extra virgin olive oil and grated Parmigiano-Reggiano cheese.

Pizza Azzuro's Grilled Shrimp with Rancho Gordo White Beans, Caggiano Sausage, and Arugula

1 cup white beans, such as Runner Cannellinis or Mayacobas, cooked, strained, and liquid reserved

6 ounces Italian sausage cut into small pieces

1 yellow onion, finely chopped

1 carrot, finely chopped

2 small celery stalks, finely chopped

1 tablespoon garlic, finely chopped

1 tablespoon butter

1 cup arugula

Salt and freshly ground black pepper to taste

1 pound medium Gulf white shrimp, shelled and de-veined

Extra virgin olive oil

SERVES 2-4
AS AN APPETIZER

On any given night in downtown Napa you'll see restaurants of all kinds filled to various degrees of capacity, except for Pizza Azzuro. It will be packed. They have great pizzas that remind me of the masterpieces I used to eat in the Trastevere district of Rome. The staff is like family and the dining room is open and inviting—and they serve this killer bean dish that makes me proud! We like to use local Caggiano sausages from Sonoma but any high-quality Italian sausage will work.

Cook the beans according to the instructions on page 150; drain and reserve the broth. In a sauté pan, cook sausage in 1 tablespoon of olive oil until slightly browned. Add onions, carrots, celery, and garlic and cook until tender. Add beans and ½ cup of the cooking liquid, cooking until heated through and mixture begins to thicken. Add butter, check for seasoning, and adjust with salt and freshly ground pepper. Add arugula and set aside.

Meanwhile, salt and pepper shrimp. Drizzle with olive oil and grill on high heat, about 2 minutes per side.

To serve, place bean and sausage mixture in a bowl and top with 5–6 grilled shrimp per person.

Globe's Warm Octopus Salad

¼ pound of Christmas Lima beans, soaked, liquid reserved

¼ cup extra virgin olive oil, plus extra for drizzling

1 tablespoon salt

2 sprigs of mint

1 pound octopus

1 bay leaf

½ onion

1 pound octopus

1 bay leaf

½ onion

1 medium to large bulb of fennel, thinly shaved

1 bunch of arugula, washed and spun

Juice of 1 orange, plus zest of ¼ orange, julienned

¼ cup cerignola olives, pitted

SERVES **4-6** AS AN APPETIZER

Despite its sophisticated, urban reputation, San Francisco's dirty little secret is that its citizens don't stay up late and like to be in bed by a comfortable hour. I don't know whether it's the fog or a dedication to daylight, but there are many complaints that the city just folds up too early. There are a few bright spots after hours and Jason Tallent has made Globe one of the late-night destinations that night owls and other chefs gravitate toward. Jason is a very clever chef and became one of my earliest customers at a time when other chefs seemed intimidated by the wild array of heirloom beans I brought to the farmers market.

With his recipe, you can substitute squid, cuttlefish, or any size octopus. This dish is fun because the color of the octopus and the color of the beans are quite the same.

Soak the beans overnight to make them tender and help retain a touch of their color contrast.

Place the beans and their soaking liquid in a medium-sized pot and bring to a simmer. When the beans are tender, turn off the heat and drain any excess water until the beans are just touching the top of the water. Add a pinch of salt, ¼ cup of olive oil, and 1 sprig of mint. Stir and let sit until the mixture has cooled to room temperature.

In a medium-sized pot filled with water, add a large pinch of salt, the bay leaf, onion, and octopus. Bring the pot to a slow simmer and let cook for about an hour and a half. The octopus should be tender but not soft if you are substituting calamari or smaller octopus your cooking time will be slightly less. After the octopus is tender, strain, reserving about ½ cup of the cooking liquid. Cut the octopus into smaller, bite-size pieces (if you want, grill it first to add some char and smoked flavor).

In a deep plate, make a bed of the beans and octopus, making sure that yummy olive oil is in there. Mix the fennel, arugula, orange zest, half the juice of the orange and a pinch of salt. Add to the top of the bean and octopus mix. Sprinkle on the olives, more mint leaves, and finish with a drizzle of, yes—more olive oil.

Norman Rose Crock

The Norman Rose Tavern is one of Napa's brightest spots. They serve great pub food and you see all walks of life come through the doors, looking for some fun and good grub. Their recipe for what they call a Crock O' Beans is a shining example of how incredible simple beans can be with the right chef (in this case, Reed Herrick) at the helm.

THE BEANS

2 cups Yellow Indian Woman beans

4 cups water

Soak beans overnight.

Preheat oven to 350 degrees F. Drain the beans and cover with new water; add 1 tablespoon sea salt and bring to a boil. Cover beans and bake for 1½ hours or until tender. Allow beans to cool in boiling liquid.

THE MIREPOIX

1 small onion, diced

2 carrots, diced

1 celery stalk, diced

1 tablespoon thyme

2 tablespoon extra virgin olive oil

1 teaspoon garlic, minced

Sauté the mirepoix ingredients until tender.

THE HERB BUTTER

3 tablespoon butter, softened

1 tablespoon parsley, finely chopped

1 tablespoon chives, finely chopped

1 tablespoon tarragon, finely chopped

Salt and freshly ground pepper to taste

Combine herbs with softened butter and set aside.

Combine the beans, mirepoix, and herb butter. Simmer for 10–15 minutes.

Salt and pepper to taste.

SERVES 4-6

Baked Salmon with Dijon and Silky Snowcaps

THE BEANS

½ pound Snowcap beans, cooked and drained

¼ cup heavy cream

2 tablespoons butter

2 sprigs fresh thyme, plus 1 tablespoon finely chopped

Kosher salt and freshly ground pepper to taste

Pinch of cayenne pepper

THE SALMON

4 (8-ounce) salmon fillets, pin bones and skin removed

2 tablespoons Dijon mustard

Kosher salt and freshly ground pepper to taste

Parmigiano-Reggiano cheese, grated, as desired

SERVES 4

It seems everyone at Rancho Gordo likes to cook. Lynn Arthur spends her time on various food-related projects, including Rancho Gordo and the very fine Osprey Fish Market in Napa. Lynn developed this recipe while working at the market, and it's a great example of the unusual but excellent combination of beans and fish.

THE BEANS

Cook the beans according to the instructions on page 150; drain. Place half the beans in a large bowl and mash, reserving the other half of whole beans.

Place cream in a heavy saucepan, bring to a low boil until reduced by half. Add thyme sprigs and let steep for 5 minutes. Remove thyme from cream.

Mix mashed beans with butter and reduced cream, until well combined. Add reserved whole beans and mix until just combined. Season to taste with salt, pepper, and cayenne.

THE SALMON

Preheat oven to 400 degrees F.

Place parchment paper on a sheet pan and oil lightly. Place the salmon skin side down on the parchment paper. Salt and pepper the fillets, then lightly brush the top of each fillet with Dijon mustard.

Bake salmon for 10–12 minutes, or slightly longer if you prefer it well-done.

To serve, place a mound of Snowcaps in the center of each plate. Grate a little Parmegiano-Reggiano over beans, then place a salmon fillet on top of the beans and sprinkle with finely chopped thyme.

Snowcap beans.

Vegetable Soup

1 cup heirloom beans, soaked,
liquid reserved

1 bay leaf

3-inch piece kombu
(sea vegetable)

1 tablespoon olive oil

1 onion, diced, or leek (white only),
cut in ¼ inch half moons

1 carrot, cut in ¼ inch half moons

1 rib celery, sliced

1 red potato, cut in ½ inch dice
(or parsnip, rutabaga or turnip)

2 cups winter squash
such as kabocha,
peeled and cut in ½ inch dice

½ teaspoon sea salt

3 cups water

1 tomato, chopped

½ cup fresh herbs, chopped

Freshly ground pepper

¼ cup white miso, light barley miso
or chickpea miso (gluten free)

Half a bunch arugula or parsley,
or cooked hearty greens
such as kale, chopped

SERVES 8

Meredith McCarty is a nutritionist and healthy food educator I discovered on the Internet (www.healingcuisine.com). She has some great classes and good ideas on food, and clearly she's an excellent cook. I always market beans as a quality ingredient worthy of the best kitchens in the world. The nutritive and ecological benefits they offer are secondary to me, because I don't believe there is a huge market for "moral food." We eat what we like or we're fighting our food.

But the reality is that beans are a superfood, and when you consider how easy it is to produce them (as compared to beef), they should be more central to our diet and meat should be the occasional treat. Anyway, moral or not, healthy or not, green or not, Meredith's soup is excellent and easy to make, and a fine example of delicious, healthy cooking.

Bring beans to a boil in their soaking liquid, lower to a simmer, and add the bay leaf and kombu. When beans are fully cooked, remove some cooking liquid and vigorously whisk the kombu to dissolve it, then add back to beans.

Heat the olive oil in a heavy 3-quart pot. Add the onion and garlic and sauté briefly until soft. Add the carrot, celery, potato, squash, salt and water to barely cover. Add the tomatoes and fresh herbs, and season with fresh ground pepper. Then add the beans and some of the bean broth and cook a couple of minutes more. In a separate bowl, dissolve miso in a little of the hot soup broth, then add to the pot. Stir in the greens and serve.

Resources

WHERE TO FIND HEIRLOOM BEANS

Alma Gourmet, Ltd.

www.almagourmet.com

Alma Gourmet is an online retailer carrying a variety of beans, including the Republic of Beans product line.

Marx Foods

www.marxfoods.com

Primarily a high-end restaurant distributor until 2007, Marx foods now has an online retail store for home chefs, offering all kinds of fine foods in bulk, including over sixteen varieties of heirloom beans and lentils.

Native Seeds/SEARCH

www.nativeseeds.org

A nonprofit conservation organization, Native Seeds/SEARCH has been collecting seeds and preserving the biodiversity of the arid Southwest for over 25 years. They currently offer over 350 varieties of seeds as well as food and other specialty products, including heirloom beans, online, in their catalogs, and in their retail store in Tucson, Arizona.

North Bay Trading Company

www.northbaytrading.com

This is a great resource for Christmas Limas, both by the pound and in bulk quantities.

Phipps Country Store

www.phippscountry.com

Phipps is an old-time country store and farm in Pescadero, CA, with an online store offering dozens of heirloom bean varieties, many of which they grow on their farm.

Purcell Mountain Farms

wwww.purcellmountainfarms.com

Purcell Mountain Farm is a family-operated farm in the foothills of the Purcell Mountains in northeastern Idaho that operates an online farm store offering more than 100 varieties of beans, as well as hominy, spices, lentils, peas, exotic rice and other grains, and chiles.

Purely American: Great Finds in Regional American Foods

www.purelyamerican.com

Under their Pioneer Harvest product line, Purely American offers 16 varieties of heirloom beans and grains from the New World at $3.95 per pound. Their website offers interesting descriptions, stories, and recipes for each bean.

Rancho Gordo

www.ranchogordo.com

We grow 25 heirloom varieties and import 10. Order onliine or visit us in Napa.

Republic of Beans

www.republicofbeans.com

The Republic of Beans carries a great array of Italian heritage beans from renowned Chef Cesare Casella, along with spices, grains and other regional specialty foods.

Seed Savers Exchange

www.seedsavers.org

Seed Savers is a nonprofit organization of gardeners that has been dedicated to saving and sharing seeds for over 30 years. Many varieties of both eating beans and heirloom seed stock can be purchased online, or through their annual catalog.

Sun Organic Farm

sunorganicfarm.com

An online organic food store, Sun Organic Farm offers 65 varieties of beans, lentils, and peas, including some heirlooms. Most are offered in bulk quantities, but some can be found in 1–3 pound increments.

WHERE TO FIND SEED STOCK FOR HEIRLOOM BEANS

Amishland Heirloom Seeds

www.amishlandseeds.com

Amishland Heirloom Seeds is a one-woman operation in Lancaster County, Pennsylvania. Lisa Von Saunders specializes in growing and collecting rare heirloom varieties of the region, and sells over 30 varieties of her own heirloom bean seed stock through her mail-order business.

Baker Creek Heirloom Seeds

www.rareseeds.com

Baker Creek Heirloom Seeds offers over 1400 varieties of heirloom seeds, including over 60 varieties of beans, in their online store, retail outlets in California and Missouri, as well as in their free catalog.

Native Seeds/SEARCH

www.nativeseeds.org

A nonprofit conservation organization, Native Seeds/SEARCH has been collecting seeds and preserving the biodiversity of the arid Southwest for over 25 years. They currently offer over 350 varieties of seeds as well as food and other specialty products, including heirloom beans, online, in their catalogs, and in their retail store in Tucson, Arizona.

Seed Savers Exchange

www.seedsavers.org

Seed Savers is a nonprofit organization of gardeners that has been dedicated to saving and sharing seeds for over 30 years. Many varieties of both eating beans and heirloom

seed stock can be purchased online, or through their annual catalog.

Sustainable Mountain Agriculture

www.heirlooms.org

Bill Best at Sustainable Mountain Agriculture has been collecting heirloom seeds, primarily beans, of the Appalachian region for over 30 years. He has collected over 400 varieties of seeds and offers over 50 varieties for mail-order sale in his annual catalog.

Terroir Seeds

www.underwoodgardens.com

Terroir Seeds offers heirloom vegetable seeds from Underwood Gardens in Chino Valley, Arizona, and features "Grandma's Garden" annual seed catalog. More than twenty varieties of heirloom been seed stock can be purchased online or through the catalog.

Foraging amaranth seeds.

For Further Reading

Albala, Ken. *Beans: A History*.
Oxford: Berg, 2007.

Ashworth, Suzanne and Kent Whealy.
*Seed to Seed: Seed Saving and Growing
Techniques for Vegetable Gardeners*.
Decorah, IA: Seed Savers Exchange, 2002.

Barrett, Judith. *Fagioli: The Bean Cuisine
of Italy*. Emmaus, PA: Rodale, 2004.

Berry, Elizabeth and Florence Fabricant.
Elizabeth Berry's Great Bean Book.
Berkeley, CA: Ten Speed, 1999.

Duke, James A. *Handbook of Legumes
of World Economic Importance*. New York:
Plenum, 1980.

Green, Aliza. *The Bean Bible: A Legumaniac's
Guide to Lentils, Peas, and Every Edible Bean
on the Planet!* Philadelphia: Running Press,
2000.

Hardenburg, E. B. *Bean Culture*.
New York: Macmillan, 1927.

Justice, Oren L. and Louis N. Bass. *Principles
and Practices of Seed Storage*. Washington:
U.S. Department of Agriculture, 1978.

Kennedy, Diana. *The Cuisines of Mexico*.
New York: Harper & Row, 1972.

Miller, Ashley, *The Bean Harvest Cookbook*.
Newtown, CT: Taunton, 1997.

Nabhan, Gary Paul, ed. *Renewing America's
Food Traditions: Saving and Savoring the
Continent's Most Endangered Foods*. White
River Junction, VT: Chelsea Green, 2008

Robertson, Lynn Shelby and Russell D.
Frazier. *Dry Bean Production: Principles
and Practices*. East Lansing, MI:
Michigan State University, 1978.

Sando, Steve and Vanessa Barrington.
*Heirloom Beans: Great Recipes for Dips
and Spreads, Soups and Stews, Salads and
Salsas, and Much More from Rancho Gordo*.
San Francisco: Chronicle, 2008.

Sass Lorna. *Whole Grains: Every Day, Every
Way*. New York: Clarkson Potter, 2006.

Sevey, Glenn C. and A. W. Fulton.
*Bean Culture: A Practical Treatise on
the Production and Marketing of Beans*.
New York: O. Judd Company, 1907.

Verrill, A. Hyatt and Otis W. Barrett.
Foods America Gave the World. Boston:
L.C. Page, 1937.

Yadva, N. D. and N. L. Vyas. *Arid Legumes*.
Bikaner, India: Agro Botanical 1994.

My overflowing bookshelves.

Conversion Tables

Volume conversions

⅛ teaspoon	0.5 milliliters
¼ teaspoon	1 milliliter
½ teaspoon	2 milliliters
1 teaspoon	5 milliliters
½ tablespoon	7 milliliters
1 tablespoon (3 teaspoons)	15 milliliters
2 tablespoons (1 fluid ounce)	30 milliliters
¼ cup (4 tablespoons)	60 milliliters
⅓ cup	90 milliliters
½ cup (4 fluid ounces)	125 milliliters
⅔ cup	160 milliliters
¾ cup (6 fluid ounces)	180 milliliters
1 cup (16 tablespoons)	250 milliliters
1 pint (2 cups)	500 milliliters
1 quart (4 cups)	1 liter (about)

Weight conversions

½ ounce	15 grams
1 ounce	30 grams
2 ounces	60 grams
3 ounces	85 grams
¼ pound (4 ounces)	115 grams
½ pound (8 ounces)	225 grams
¾ pound (12 ounces)	340 grams
1 pound (16 ounces)	454 grams

To convert length:	Multiply by:
Inches to centimeters	2.54
Inches to millimeters	25.4
Feet to centimeters	30.5
Yards to meters	0.9
Miles to kilometers	1.6
Miles to meters	1609.3

Oven temperature conversions

DEGREES FAHRENHEIT	DEGREES CELSIUS
200 degrees F	100 degrees C
250 degrees F	120 degrees C
275 degrees F	140 degrees C
300 degrees F	150 degrees C
325 degrees F	160 degrees C
350 degrees F	180 degrees C
375 degrees F	190 degrees C
400 degrees F	200 degrees C
425 degrees F	220 degrees C
450 degrees F	230 degrees C

Cactus and prickly pears.

Acknowledgments

First and foremost I need to thank Neal Maillet, formerly of Timber Press, who seemed to understand the work I'm doing more than most. He's a good guy to have on your team. The entire Timber family has been helpful and thanks are due to Juree Sondker and Eve Goodman. Carolyn Holland is a wonderful copyeditor who made me sound more intelligent than I am and photographer Emma Alpaugh is a raw bean's best friend.

Katherine Cowles is my literary agent and friend and I wish every writer was lucky enough to have a Katherine as an advocate and friend. My staff here at Rancho Gordo has been patient and I know full well that they all are a key part of Rancho Gordo's success. General manager Susan Sanchez keeps the whole machine running strong. Thanks also to my mother, Mary Lee.

Thanks to Eileen Pharo (gardening), Colby Eierman (trellising), and Louisa Hufstader (botany) for their help in preparing this book.

Most importantly, I want to thank the growers, here and in Latin America, who know the importance of beans and help me to tell a good story.

STEVE SANDO

Index

About the Author

In a few short years, Steve Sando has taken the lowly bean from a neglected legume to superstar-status ingredient. Sando's company, Rancho Gordo, grows, imports, and promotes heirloom and heritage varieties while working directly with consumers and chefs like Thomas Keller, Deborah Madison, Paula Wolfert, and David Kinch.

Sando's seed saving, bean production, and marketing efforts provide professional and home chefs with heirloom beans that would otherwise have been lost to history. The beans, along with corn, chiles, and tomatoes, have become key ingredients in the new American food revolution centered in Sando's native San Francisco Bay Area. In fact, Sando and Rancho Gordo were named number two on *Saveur Magazine*'s "The Saveur 100 list for 2008." *Bon Appetit* magazine declared Sando one of the Hot 10 in the food world of 2009. *Food + Wine* magazine placed Steve "at the forefront of the current seed-saving movement." Steve's previous book, with Vanessa Barrington, was *Heirloom Beans* (Chronicle 2008).

Steve Sando came to agriculture not from the 4H club but from the grocery store. As a frustrated home cook, he decided to grow the ingredients he wanted in his kitchen. At the forefront of neglected ingredients were beans. Although they are an indigenous product of the Americas, the only beans available commercially to most home cooks were pintos, navys, and kidneys. Discovering heirloom beans to be as rich and varied as heirloom tomatoes, Sando almost singlehandedly created the market for these unique and worthwhile legumes. He now grows more than 25 varieties in California and works with small indigenous farmers in Mexico to import their heirloom beans for the U.S. market. He lives in Napa and travels frequently throughout the Americas collecting beans, friends, and adventures.